Making New Choices

"Your time is precious, too precious to waste feeling unhappy. Life is meant to be lived; each day should be a joy, not a struggle. It should be like strolling through a field on a sunny day, not battling through a neverending storm," the old man said.

"What do you mean?" the young man asked. "People don't choose to be unhappy. It all depends upon their circumstances, it's what happens to someone that makes them happy or unhappy."

"I don't believe that your circumstances, whatever they may be, have any power to make you feel happy or unhappy," said the old man. "It is only your opinion about your circumstances that determines how you feel."

BY ADAM J. JACKSON

The Secrets of Abundant Health
The Secrets of Abundant Wealth
The Secrets of Abundant Love

To be published by HarperPaperbacks

The TEN SECRETS of ABUNDANT HAPPINESS

*A Modern Parable of Wisdom
and Happiness That Will
Change Your Life*

ADAM J. JACKSON

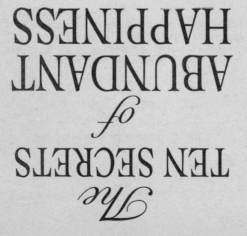

HarperPaperbacks
A Division of HarperCollinsPublishers

HarperPaperbacks   *A Division of* HarperCollins*Publishers*
10 East 53rd Street, New York, N.Y. 10022

A trade paperback edition of this book was published in 1996 in Great Britain by Thorsons, an imprint of HarperCollins*Publishers*.

Cover and interior illustrations by Joan Perrin Falquet

First HarperPaperbacks printing: July 1996

Printed in the United States of America

HarperPaperbacks and colophon are trademarks of HarperCollins*Publishers*

❖ 10 9 8 7 6 5 4 3 2 1

For my wife, Karen,
and my children, Sophie and Samuel
with love always.

Contents

Acknowledgments

I would like to thank all those people who have helped me in my work and in the writing of this book. I am particularly grateful to:

My literary agent, Sara Menguc, and her assistant, Georgia Glover, for all their efforts and work on my behalf.

Everyone at Thorsons, but especially Erica Smith for her enthusiasm and constructive comments throughout the writing of the book, and Fiona Brown who edited the manuscript.

My mother, who always encouraged me to write, and remains a constant source of inspiration and love to me; my father for his encouragement, guidance and help in all my work, and all of my family and friends for their love.

And finally, to Karen—my wife, my best friend, and my most candid editor. Words cannot express my love for the one person who has always had faith in me and believed in my work.

Introduction

> You traverse the world in search of happiness,
> which is in the reach of every man
> —*Horace*

Ask people what they most want from life, and the answer you most commonly hear is: "I just want to be happy." Why is it then that so few people are happy? Why is it that one of the biggest growth areas in the drug industry is anti-depressants? Why is it that the number of people who consider themselves to be happy is so small? Could it be that we have been looking for happiness in the wrong places?

I believe that we all have the power to be happy. It does not matter how much money you do or don't have, what job you do, or where you live. Whatever your circumstances are at this moment, you have the power not just to be happy, but to experience happiness in abundance.

Abundant Happiness is not just a matter of being free from depression and misery, it is rather a feeling of joy, contentment, and wonderment for life. This does not mean that it is possible or even desirable to be in a continual state of ecstasy; after all, there are times when personal tragedies and loss touch our lives and lead quite naturally to sadness, grief, and disappointment. But there are ways through which we can cope and deal with those experiences, and often we can turn the challenges and adversities of life into triumph.

Unlike most parables, all of the characters in this book are based upon real people (with the exception of the old Chinese man who is based upon a composite of several wise old men and women I have met). I have, of course, changed their names and modified their circumstances to hopefully benefit the story, but nevertheless they all triumphed over their personal crises and found personal happiness as recorded in each chapter. It is my hope that their stories will uplift and inspire you to follow their example and experience the blessings of Abundant Happiness in your own life.

Adam Jackson
Hertfordshire
March 1995

The DRIVER

It all began one cold and wet October evening on his way home from work. It was 8 P.M., the third time that week he'd had to stay late at the office. The sky had been overcast all day and the heavens had decided to let loose a torrential downpour just as the young man had set off on his journey home. A question on the radio interrupted his thoughts. It was a simple question, one which the young man had never really consciously asked himself, and the answers to which it led disturbed him.

The question had been prompted by a national survey which found that only one person in 50 considered themselves to be happy or contented, and less than one person in 10 could remember a time— even a moment—when they had been truly happy. It was a simple, straightforward question that the radio presenter asked his listeners: "Are you happy?"

The question caused the young man to suddenly reflect upon his own life. He lacked nothing to speak of: he was in reasonable health, he had a good job, he always somehow managed to pay the bills and occasionally put a little aside for minor luxuries. He had a close circle of friends and a loving family. But despite all this, he felt empty inside, disillusioned with life. Something was missing; he didn't know what it was, all he knew was that something was missing from his life. There were many words he could have used to describe his life, but "happy" was definitely not one of them.

It was Thoreau who said, "Most people live their lives in quiet desperation," and the young man thought that this was a fair description of his own existence. Each day seemed, from beginning to end, to be a struggle; one day converging into the next, with the same or similar frustrations and the same stresses. He couldn't help feeling that his life had turned into an endless, monotonous cycle. What had happened to all his boyhood hopes and dreams? Where was the passion and joy he knew as a child? When had it all begun to be such a struggle?

He had read somewhere that some religious philosophies taught that life was a continuous struggle, but the young man couldn't accept it. "Surely," he told himself, "there has to be more to life than this?" He felt confused, lost, as if trapped inside a giant labyrinth, not knowing how he had got there and unsure of the way out.

At that moment, the young man's thoughts were interrupted; but this time by smoke rising from under the bonnet of the car.

"Damn! If it's not one thing, it's another," he muttered to himself as he pulled the car to the edge of the highway. He got out of the car, lifted up the bonnet to take a look at the engine, and was hit full in the face by a gush of piercing steam that almost knocked him backward.

He raised his jacket over his head, hunched over to protect himself from the wind and rain, and walked one and a half kilometres along the highway to the nearest telephone and called the breakdown service for help. The operator advised him that a service mechanic would be with him within an hour or so. There was nothing he could do but return to his car and wait.

A question echoed in his head: "What is the point of it all? What is the point?"

There was no answer, of course. He didn't expect one. All he could hear was the sound of the traffic passing him by.

And so, cold, tired, and miserable, the young man wearily walked back to his car. He was not aware that this event was to mark the beginning of one of the most profound changes in his life. Had he known what was to follow, there is no doubt—and he would freely confess this in later years—he would have smiled and known the feeling of Abundant Happiness.

The MEETING

As the young man approached his car, he noticed a man leaning against it. A curious-looking character; an old Chinese man in white overalls, wearing a bright yellow baseball cap. He was a small man with a kindly, lined face and long, flowing white hair, but what the young man noticed most about the old man was his eyes. They were very deep, dark brown, smiling eyes.

The old man was smiling as the young man approached. "A wonderful storm, no?" he said.

"Cold, wet, and miserable, if you ask me," muttered the young man.

But the old Chinese man continued undeterred by the young man's mutterings. "Do you feel the energy? Can you smell the freshness in the air? Doesn't it make you feel wonderful?"

"Not really," the young man thought to himself, but stayed silent. He took a closer look at this peculiar old man. The storm had passed only a minute or so before he arrived back at the car and it was still drizzling but the old man was not wet at all. There was not one drop of rain on him. But before the young man had time to comment, the old man spoke.

"So, what took you?" he said.

"What do you mean? I was told I would have to wait an hour for someone to arrive," replied the young man.

"Well, life's full of surprises," said the old man with a broad grin. "So, what's the problem?"

"I'm not sure what's wrong," explained the young man. "I was driving along when smoke started rising out of the bonnet and the engine just cut out."

"Okay, let's take a good look," said the old man and he rolled up his sleeves, stepped forward, and began to examine the engine.

After a few minutes the old man looked up and turned to the young man and smiled. "You don't need to look so worried. It's nothing that can't be fixed," he said.

"Thank goodness for that," said the young man with a sigh of relief.

"It might cost you a few thousand pounds ... but it definitely can be fixed!" said the old man.

"Oh, no. You've got to be joking!" exclaimed the young man.

The old man patted the young man on the arm and laughed. "Of course I am."

The old man turned around to pick up a spanner but stopped briefly as he met the young man's gaze, and then turned back to the engine. "It might never happen, you know."

"What?"

"Whatever it is that's troubling you."

"Nothing is troubling me," said the young man.

"Ah . . . I see. That's good then," said the old man, and he picked up a screwdriver and began whistling a tune as he continued working on the car.

"It sounds like you've had a good day," said the young man.

"Of course. When you reach my age," said the old man, "every day that you are above the ground is a good day!" He turned around to face the young man."If you ask me, life is simply too short and too precious to waste feeling miserable. Did you know that the average life is 76 years? That is just 3,952 weeks! And 1,317 of those weeks you will spend asleep. That leaves just 2,635 weeks or 63,240 hours of living!

"How old are you?" asked the old man.

"Thirty-three."

"So, that means that, if you are fortunate enough to live an average life, you have only about 1,114 weeks left to live!"

"Well, that is a cheerful thought!" said the young man in a blatantly sarcastic tone.

"It simply shows you that your time is precious, too precious to waste feeling unhappy. Life is meant to be lived; each day should be a joy not a struggle. It should be like strolling through a field on a sunny day, not battling through a neverending storm."

The young man felt a shiver run down his spine and the hairs on the back of his neck rise. How did the old man know how he was feeling? He tried to reassure himself that it was just a coincidence, after all, the old man could not possibly know what he was thinking.

"It always surprises me that so many people choose to be unhappy," said the old man as he turned back to his work on the car engine. The young man leaned against the side of the car.

"What do you mean?" he said. "People don't *choose* to be unhappy. It all depends upon their circumstances, it's what happens to someone that makes them happy or unhappy."

"Of course, you may be right. But, if your happiness was determined solely by your circumstances, why is it that another person can experience the same tragedies or joys as you, but react and feel completely differently about it? I once knew two men who were both badly injured in the same car accident. One became depressed but the other was remarkably cheerful."

"Why were their reactions so different?" asked the young man.

"The depressed man was bitter and repeatedly asked, 'Why did it have to happen to me?' whereas the cheerful man said, 'Thank God I am still alive!' It's like the poem: 'Two men looked out between closed bars, one saw mud, the other stars.'"

"I don't believe that your circumstances, whatever they may be, have any power to make you feel happy or unhappy," said the old man. "It is only your opinion about your circumstances that determines how you feel. After all, who is happier, the man who sees his cup as half full, or the man who sees his cup as half empty? Ah ha ... found it. Could you pass me that wrench?" he said, holding his hand out behind his back to the young man.

"Here you are," said the young man, "but surely something either makes you feel happy or it doesn't?"

The old man put down his wrench and turned, resting against the car and faced the young man. "So, what would make you happy?" he asked.

The young man thought for a moment. "I'm not sure. I suppose more money would help for a start," he said.

The old man turned back to the young man whilst getting another tool from his toolbox. "Do you really believe that money brings happiness?" he asked.

"I'm not sure, but at least it allows you to be miserable in comfort," said the young man, breaking into a smile.

"Good point," admitted the old man with a grin. "But, comfortable misery is still misery! You may be in more comfortable surroundings, but you will feel just as uncomfortable as if you had nothing. If money brought happiness, millionaires would be the happiest people in the world, but we all know that the rich know misery and depression just as well as the poor. All money can buy is material possessions—like your car here—but these are temporary distractions, they cannot bring you lasting happiness."

The young man looked away, thinking about what the old man had said, and the old man picked up a spanner and went back to repairing the car.

"What about a different job?" said the young man. "I think I would be happier if I had a different career."

"Now you're beginning to sound like the stonecutter!" said the old man with a laugh.

"What do you mean—stonecutter?"

"In my country, there is a story of a stonecutter who was unhappy and wished to be someone else with a different position in life.

"One day, he passed a wealthy merchant's house and saw all of the great possessions the merchant possessed and he noticed how well-respected the merchant was about the town. The stonecutter was envious of this great merchant and wished he could be exactly like him. Then he would no longer have to be a mere stonecutter.

"To his astonishment, his wish was granted and he suddenly became the merchant, and had more power and more luxuries than he had ever dreamed of. He was also envied and despised by the poorer people and had more enemies than he had dreamed of as well.

"Then he noticed a high official being transported by servants and surrounded by soldiers. Everyone bowed to the great and mighty official. He was more powerful and respected than any other throughout the kingdom. And the stonecutter, who was now a merchant, wished he could be like the high official, with servants and soldiers to guard him and more power than any other.

"His wish was again granted and he became the high official, the most powerful man in all the kingdom, before whom everyone bowed. But the official was the most feared and hated in all the kingdom as well, which is why he needed so many soldiers to guard him, and the heat of the sun made the official very uncomfortable and weary. He looked up at the fierce sun shining brightly in the sky and said, 'How powerful it is, I wish I could be the sun.'

"And no sooner had he wished it than he became the sun, shining down on the earth. But a big black cloud came along and blocked the sun's rays. 'How mighty the cloud is,' he thought, 'I wish I was as powerful as the cloud.'

"Then he became the cloud covering the sun's rays and raining down on the villages. But a mighty wind came and blew the cloud away. 'I wish I could be as powerful as the wind,' he thought, and as he said it, so he became the wind.

"But whilst the wind could uproot trees and destroy whole villages, it was powerless against a great boulder. The huge stone was unmovable, resisting all force of the wind. 'How powerful the stone is,' he said. 'How I wish I could be as powerful as stone.'

"Then he became the great stone which resisted the most powerful wind. He was now happy at last—the most powerful force of everything on the earth. But then he heard a noise. Chink. Chink. Chink. Chink. A hammer was banging a chisel into the stone, breaking it away, piece by piece. 'What could be more powerful than I?' he thought, and there at the foot of the great stone was . . . a stonecutter.

"Many people spend their whole lives in search of happiness, and never find it simply because they look in the wrong place. You won't see a sunset if you're facing east and you won't find happiness searching amongst the things around you. The story of the stonecutter teaches that you cannot find happiness by changing anything in your life . . . except yourself."

"But I still don't understand," said the young man.

"What about personal tragedies and disappoint-ments? How can someone still be happy in those cir-cumstances?"

"Each of us is like a ship," continued the old man, "traveling across the sea of life. Winds and storms—natural disasters, personal tragedies—will come and go, but so long as you control your rudder and sails, you can travel wherever you please, regardless of those storms and winds. In fact, storms and rain can enrich life; it depends on how you look at them."

"I'm not with you," said the young man.

"Storms clear the air and bring rain, and what would life be without rain? There would be no growth, no richness in life, and there would be no rainbows. Storms bring winds, and if you know how to sail your ship, you can always use the power of the wind to your advantage."

"I can see how it fits into your analogy, but I don't agree. How can an adversity be turned into an advan-tage?" interrupted the young man.

"You have heard that every cloud has a silver lining?"

"Yes, of course. But that's just a saying. I've never found a tragedy to be an advantage."

"Perhaps that is because you have never looked for it. There is no problem that does not bring with it a gift. Everything that happens has a purpose, a reason, and a lesson that can enrich your life. Many people drift through life, slaves to circumstances and ruled by the storms and winds because they do not realize that they have a rudder and sails, let alone how to use them. They have forgotten how to sail their ship and so they blame the weather. They do not realize that, whatever their circumstances, they can still choose to be happy."

"But you can't choose *all* your feelings," persisted the young man.

"Whatever you sincerely believe is, for you, true," said the old man. "You must therefore think carefully about what you choose to believe!"

"Come on, now," argued the young man. "Surely you're not saying that you believe anyone, whatever their circumstances, can be happy? What about a person who is crippled or blind or deaf and dumb? How can such a person be happy?"

"Obviously you have never met anyone who is handicapped," said the old man. "I know it seems strange, to think that someone who has fewer advantages in life than you can be happy when you are not, but it's nevertheless true. Do you know what Helen Keller—who was blind, deaf, and dumb throughout her life—said when asked what her life had been like with such severe handicaps?"

The young man shook his head.

"She said," continued the old man, "'My life has been so beautiful,' and the great writer Milton who was himself blind explained, 'It is not miserable to be blind. It is only miserable not to be able to endure blindness.' Similarly, wealth, health, fame, and power are no guarantee of happiness. When Napoleon, the emperor of the French empire and one of the most powerful men in the world of his time, was asked if his life had been happy, he answered, 'I have not known more than six days of happiness.'"

The young man was amazed. "What is the explanation? How can someone with such terrible handicaps be so happy and someone who has so much power and wealth be so unhappy?"

The old man finished his work on the car and turned to face the young man.

"Happiness is one of the greatest gifts of life, and it is available to everybody. You see, you don't find happiness, you create it. And, whatever your circumstances, you have the power to create your own happiness."

"How can you create happiness?" asked the young man.

"The universe is governed by laws, precise laws which control the natural order of things. From the motion of the waves to the rising and setting of the sun, to the timing of the seasons, everything in Nature is governed by laws. Scientists have discovered many of these laws—laws of gravity, laws of motion, laws of magnetism. But there are also laws which are not as well known, and among them are the laws of happiness."

"Laws of happiness?" asked the perplexed young man, "What are they?"

"They are 10 timeless principles which, if followed, cannot fail to create happiness. Throughout the ages, civilizations discarded these laws in their search for great wealth and, in time, the laws were forgotten, known only to those few people who remained faithful to them. And so they came to be known as 'secrets'."

"How can I find out about them?" asked the young man.

"One moment . . . nearly done. There you are . . . finished. Good as new," said the old man, wiping his hands on a cloth. "You will find out soon enough. Here, take this," he said, handing a piece of paper to the young man.

The young man looked at the piece of paper; it contained no secrets, no laws, no aphorisms—just a list of 10 names and 10 telephone numbers. He turned the paper over expecting to find something on the other side, but it was blank.

"What is this? Where are the secrets?" but when he looked up, the old man was no longer there. "Hey!" he shouted, walking around the car. "Where are you? This is just a list of names!" He looked up and down the highway but the old man was nowhere to be seen.

Just then a pick-up truck began flashing the young man and slowly pulled up behind his car. The young man walked briskly up to the driver's door.

"How in the name of heaven did you . . . ?" He stopped mid-sentence. It was not the old man.

"What's the problem?" said the mechanic as he climbed down.

"Hold on a minute," said the young man. "Where's the old man?"

"What old man? What are you talking about?" said the bemused mechanic. "You reported a breakdown, didn't you?"

"Yes, but a man has already been and fixed it . . . the old Chinese man."

"What old Chinese man? Let me call back to the breakdown operator and see what has happened. Perhaps there's been a mix-up. It wouldn't surprise me. It happens now and then; the operators get so busy that they send the same report to two mechanics."

The mechanic climbed back into his van and radioed the service operator. A few minutes later he got back out. "Well, they definitely only gave your report to me. It's all on the computer. Apparently I'm the only mechanic on duty in this area this evening. Anyway, I'd better check the car for you whilst I'm here. Turn on the engine will you."

The engine turned over immediately and was running smoothly. The mechanic held up his hand signaling for the young man to turn the engine off.

"All seems fine," he said. "I can't see any problem."

Ten minutes after the mechanic had left, the young man was still sitting in his car wondering about the old Chinese man. Who was he? Where had he come from? What were the secrets of happiness of which he had spoken?

A few more minutes passed before the young man started the engine and resumed his journey home again. There were no answers to his questions; all he had was a piece of paper containing a list of 10 names and phone numbers.

The POWER of ATTITUDE

The young man began making telephone calls to the people on the old man's list as soon as he arrived home. He managed to speak to six of them. The other four were out but he left messages for them to return his call. One strange thing he noticed as he talked to the people on the list was that they all seemed to become very animated and excited when he mentioned the old Chinese man. He arranged to meet each of them in turn over the following weeks.

The first person on the young man's list was a man by the name of Barry Kesterman. Mr. Kesterman was a teacher and worked at the local school. He was teaching classes until 5 P.M. the following day but he gladly agreed to meet with the young man afterward.

Mr. Kesterman was still relatively young in

appearance; the young man thought he was probably in his late thirties or early forties, certainly no older. Mr. Kesterman was marking his students' papers when the young man knocked on his classroom door.

"Ah! Come in, come in," Mr. Kesterman said warmly, shaking the young man's hand. "It's a pleasure to meet you. Please take a seat.

"So you met the old man yesterday," said Mr. Kesterman.

"Yes. He fixed my car."

"My goodness. He certainly pops up in the most unexpected places. And he told you about the secrets of Abundant Happiness?" Mr. Kesterman said.

"Yes. You know of them?" asked the young man.

"Yes. Of course."

"And do they really work?" asked the young man.

"Most definitely. Fifteen years ago I reached one of the lowest points in my life; I had just lost my job, I was living in a small bedsit 500 kilometers from my home town, I hadn't made many friends, and I felt utterly depressed, almost despondent. It was like being engulfed in a black cloud—I just couldn't see a way forward.

"I went to the park and just sat down on a bench overlooking the lake and mulled over all my problems in my head. After a few minutes I turned round to find I was no longer alone—there was an old Chinese man sitting next to me."

The young man could hardly believe what he was hearing. A small tingling sensation ran up his spine.

"Do you mind if I make notes?" he asked.

"No. Not at all," said Mr. Kesterman, and he continued his story. "It was probably obvious that something was troubling me, but I got the impression that the old man knew exactly what my problems were, as if he could see inside me.

"We talked for a while; he told me that he was on his way to visit a friend who was feeling depressed. 'My friend has simply forgotten the golden rule of Abundant Happiness,' he said. I had never heard of any golden rule of happiness—abundant or otherwise, but then he explained: 'It is very simple,' he said. 'You are as happy as you have made up your mind to be.'

"I didn't really understand it at the time, but I later found that it is absolutely true, and I can honestly say that that simple statement is one of the most important lessons I learned in life. It encapsulates the first secret of Abundant Happiness . . . the power of your attitude."

The young man listened intently as Mr. Kesterman continued.

"Let me explain. Like most people, I had always thought things *made* me happy, but the truth is we can choose to be happy. I remember once seeing a hypnotist in a stage show. People were hypnotized on stage and were given a raw onion. They were all told that the onion was the most delicious fruit they had ever tasted. All of them bit into their onion and licked their lips with relish, savoring every mouthful. They were then given a ripe peach and told that it was a raw turnip. This time, as they bit into the peach, they immediately spat it out in disgust. It was the *attitude* which they acquired under hypnosis that determined their reaction to the onion and the peach.

"You see, the problem is, as we go through life, we often acquire negative attitudes and these are the real culprits that make us unhappy."

"What sort of negative attitudes?" interjected the young man.

"Well, a good example is what we expect from life. For instance, I was always taught that we should expect the worst, because then we won't be disappointed."

"Yes, I was taught that as well. It seems logical," said the young man.

"It's a common belief," said Mr. Kesterman, "but it's a false one, and one that most often destroys our dreams and prevents us from experiencing happiness."

"How can that be?" said the young man. "If you expect the worst and it happens, you won't be disappointed; but if it doesn't happen, you'll be pleasantly surprised. If you hope for the best, you are only setting yourself up for disappointment."

"I know it seems that way, doesn't it? But, I can demonstrate to you right now—prove to you—that if you expect the worst, you will invariably experience the worst, and vice versa.

"Take a good look around this room right now and try to notice everything that's brown."

The young man looked around the room. There were a number of things that were brown: the wooden picture frames; the light brown settee; the curtain frame; the desks, books, and numerous other small items in the room.

"Okay," said Mr. Kesterman, "Now close your eyes . . . "

The young man closed his eyes.

". . . and tell me everything you saw . . . that was . . . blue!"

The young man smiled. "I didn't notice anything blue."

"Open your eyes," said Mr. Kesterman. "See, there's blue all around you."

And there was too: a blue vase; a blue photoframe; a blue paisley pattern in the carpet; a blue letter holder on the desk; blue books on the bookshelves, and Mr. Kesterman was even wearing a blue shirt. The more he looked for blue, the more and more things he noticed which were blue.

"Look at all the things you missed!"

"But you tricked me," said the young man. "I was looking for brown objects, not blue."

"That is my point, entirely!" said Mr. Kesterman. "You were looking for brown and so you saw brown— and missed all the blue. This is what you do in life; you look for the worst and so you see the worst and miss out on the best. This is precisely what your belief of expecting or anticipating the worst leads to . . . it makes us lose sight of all the *good* things in our life.

"This is one of the reasons why many rich and famous people—people who have everything you could possibly imagine—still manage to get depressed and become drug addicts and alcoholics. They focus on what they *haven't* got instead of every-thing they *have* got, and therefore they only 'see' what is lacking in their life. In this way, they create their own misery.

"Similarly, many people who live a very modest existence are very happy because they focus on what they have got. This is why a person who regards his glass as half full will be happier than a person who regards his glass as half empty.

"You see, contrary to popular belief, everything external to us—money, cars, possessions, fame and fortune—is irrelevant. It is our attitude to life that determines our happiness in life. Therefore, to experience happiness, we don't need to have more money or a bigger house or a better job, <u>all we need to do is change our attitude</u>. This is what led Samuel Johnson to write:

> The fountain of content must <u>spring up from the mind</u>; and he who has so little knowledge of human nature as to seek happiness by <u>changing</u> anything but his <u>own disposition</u>, will waste his life in fruitless efforts and multiply the grief which he proposes to remove.

"I had never thought of it that way," said the young man. "But I suppose it makes sense."

"It's interesting, isn't it? Also, consider what generally tends to happen if you are about to do something when anticipating the worst," said Mr. Kesterman.

"What do you mean?" asked the young man.

"Well, let's say for instance, that you are about to give a speech in front of hundreds of people. You might be nervous and start thinking of all the worst things that could happen; for instance, you might forget what you were going to say, you might stutter and stammer, and you could end up making a complete fool of yourself in front of all those people. If you think these thoughts, how is that going to prepare or motivate you to do the speech? Is it going to make you feel confident or will it make you feel even more nervous?"

"I'd feel more nervous," admitted the young man.

"Of course you would, who wouldn't? And the same principle applies to everything we do in life. Who is more likely to jump out of bed in the morning eager to face the day; the person who expects that the worst things might happen in the day ahead or the person who anticipates a fantastic day? And which of them is more likely to enjoy the day?"

"I see your point, but what happens when things don't meet your expectations? What happens when bad things occur?"

"Remember the golden rule: you choose how you feel! You can look for the blue or the brown in any situation. You can focus on what's good about a situation rather than on what might appear bad."

"What if there is nothing good?"

"Sometimes, of course, when tragedies touch our lives, what seeds of goodness there are may be difficult to see. But one way to cope with tragedy is to find something positive, something meaningful in our grief. Perhaps the greatest of tragedies is when a parent suffers the heartbreak of losing a child, and in many such instances, the only way we are able to overcome our grief is to create something positive.

"For instance, one young Californian mother was devastated by the loss of her 13-year-old daughter who had been killed by a drunk driver in a road-traffic accident. When the mother discovered that the driver had a history of drunk-driving offenses and that the law was not protecting the public from him and others like him, she initiated a nationwide campaign to do something about it. Mothers Against Drunk Drivers successfully lobbied Congress and was responsible for over 950 anti-drunk-driving laws. The campaign soon spread to Canada, the United Kingdom, and New Zealand and has since saved hundreds and thousands of lives. And it all began because one woman decided to turn her grief and her loss into something positive.

"There is no experience in life that does not bring with it a gift—something that can benefit our lives and those around us, we just have to *choose* to look for it. For instance, when I met the old Chinese man all those years ago, I had lost my job, and all I could think about was that I was a failure and might never get another job. But after a long discussion with the old man that day, I began to see that losing my job might be something very positive."

"How can losing your job be positive?" asked the young man.

"For a start, it was an opportunity for me to start a new career, something that I would really believe in," said Mr. Kesterman. "So, instead of feeling depressed about losing my job, I began to feel excited, enthused, and optimistic. If you remember one thing today, remember this:

It is the meaning that we attach to the events in our lives—not the events themselves—that determine our feelings about them.

"With this attitude, losing my job represented a new beginning, a turning point in my life. When I was honest with myself, I knew that I had never really been enthused about my job. It was just a means of earning a living. But then I had a chance to think about what I really wanted to do with my life. I wanted to be able to make a difference, to have an impact—a positive impact—and make a real contribution to the community. I decided that I really wanted to be a teacher and it didn't take long for me to decide that I would go back to college.

"Let me give you another good example," said Mr. Kesterman. "Imagine that you split up from your girlfriend; you could decide it means that you are unattractive, unlovable, and will never find another girlfriend. You might think that even if you did meet someone, you would never be able to make another relationship last. Alternatively, you could reframe the situation and decide that splitting up from your girlfriend is an opportunity for you to find someone better, someone who is more suited to you. You see, it all depends upon your attitude.

"You can reframe most experiences in life to have a positive meaning. In some parts of the world even death is considered to be a time for celebration because they believe that, when we die, the soul returns to its real home and that we will all meet up with our loved ones in another time and place."

"But it's not always easy to see a positive side to a situation," insisted the young man.

"Only if you don't look for it! If you can't see a positive side, it generally means you're not searching for it. We can also help create a positive attitude by asking ourselves positive questions. Instead of asking "Why did this have to happen to me?" you can ask, 'What can I learn or how can I benefit from this experience?'"

"I'm not sure what you mean," said the young man.

"All day long you are asking yourself questions," explained Mr. Kesterman, "about the things you see, things you hear, things you smell, things you have to do, things you did and things you are doing. From when you get up in the morning to when you go to bed at night, your subconscious is constantly asking questions. In fact, the process of thought is nothing but a series of questions. Questions lead to answers and answers produce feelings. Therefore, if you feel unhappy or depressed, it usually means you are asking the wrong questions. You are asking yourself what is wrong with your life instead of what is right with it.

"Most people, when faced with a difficult situation, will ask themselves questions like: 'Why did this happen to me?' or 'What am I going to do?' These are negative, disempowering questions that produce negative, disempowering answers and create feelings of self-pity, hopelessness, and depression. If instead we asked positive, empowering questions we would produce completely different feelings."

"What questions are empowering?" asked the young man.

"Those that create feelings of power and hope. For instance, whenever I find myself in a difficult situation I consciously ask myself three powerful questions that instantly change the way I look at the situation.

"The first question is: 'What is great about this situation?'"

"But what if nothing is great?" interrupted the young man.

"Then I ask: 'What could be great about it?' You see, that question makes you look for something great in the situation and, invariably, you'll find something just as you only noticed the blue things in this room when you consciously looked for them.

"This is what is meant by the saying that every cloud has a silver lining and that every problem is merely a gift in disguise. Everything can be reframed and, in doing so, you have the power to enrich your life through every experience—this is the first secret of Abundant Happiness.

"The old man gave me a list of people, all of whom taught me about the secrets of Abundant Happiness and many of whom had suffered crises in their lives, but they all rose above their troubles because they had learned how to reframe every situation with a positive meaning.

"The second question is: 'What is not perfect yet?' This presupposes that things will be perfect and creates a different feeling than asking, 'What's wrong?'

"The third question is: 'What can I do to make things the way I want them to be, and have fun in the process?' This question helps you find all the things which are within your power to remedy the situation and also how to make the process enjoyable.

"Let me give you a few examples of how these questions work. When your car broke down yesterday evening, if you had asked, 'What's great about this situation?' you may have come up with 'It's great that I'm not hurt' or 'It's great that there's a breakdown service who will help me' or 'It's great that I didn't break down on a country lane miles from anywhere.'

"Then by asking, 'What's not perfect yet?' the answer in this case is obviously, 'My car.' And then, 'What can I do to remedy the situation and have fun in the process?' Once you've called the breakdown service and are waiting for the mechanic, you could use the time to leisurely read the newspaper or a book, or listen to a program on the radio that you never usually get a chance to hear. You could use the time creatively—plan your next holiday, write a letter, or start writing that book you've always been promising yourself that you'd write (assuming you've got pen and paper), or you could simply lie back and take a well-earned nap until the mechanic arrived.

"Another example as well: imagine you're depressed because you're overweight. What's great? It's great that you have finally reached the point that you are unhappy about your weight and really want to change. It's great that you're aware of the need to change because being overweight increases your risk of heart disease. What's not perfect yet? Your weight and shape. What are you willing to do to remedy the situation? Learn about what causes obesity, change your eating habits, and start exercising. And how can you enjoy the process of slimming? Join a slimming club so you can meet other people with the same problem, or find an exercise class that you enjoy, perhaps even take up dancing which is a great form of exercise. Find healthy foods that you enjoy and learn to cook healthy, low-fat meals."

"This is fascinating," said the young man. "So people can consciously change their attitudes by expecting the best, focusing on what is good in their lives, and asking empowering questions?"

"Absolutely," answered Mr. Kesterman. "But the essence of creating a healthy, happy attitude to life can be summarized in one word—gratitude! One of the surest secrets of Abundant Happiness is simply to cultivate an attitude of gratitude."

"And how do you do that?"

"Look for things to be grateful for," replied Mr. Kesterman. "Ask yourself every day, 'What do I have to be grateful for?'"

"But what if there is nothing to be grateful for?" persisted the young man.

Mr. Kesterman looked at the young man with raised eyebrows. "A few years ago I visited an old friend who was dying. The doctors had given him less than a year to live. I expected him to be depressed but instead found him to be not just cheerful, but positively joyous."

"How can a man with less than a year to live feel joyous?" asked the bemused young man.

"I asked him myself. 'Why are you so happy, Jim?' I said. And he said, 'Because I woke up this morning and today I'm alive!' I found his answer humbling. If a dying man can find things to be grateful for, how much more should the rest of us find?

"No matter how bad our circumstances," continued Mr. Kesterman, "there is always something—and usually many things—that we can all find to be grateful for.

"The difference between a person who lives a magical life and a person who lives a mundane life lies not in their circumstances—it lies in their attitudes. Attitude is the paintbrush of the mind with which we color our lives. We can choose whatever colors we wish."

On his way home the young man reflected upon what he had learned. He could see now that he had a lot to learn about himself and his life, but more importantly, he was beginning to understand why he had felt so unhappy for so long.

That evening the young man read the brief notes he had made at the meeting with Mr. Kesterman.

The first secret of Abundant Happiness—the power of attitude.

The foundation of my happiness begins with my attitude to life.

I am as happy as I have made up my mind to be. From now on I will make up my mind to be happy.

If I expect the best, very often I'll get it!

Happiness is a choice that I can make any time, any place, and anywhere.

Every experience can be "framed" to have a positive meaning. From now on, I will look for something positive in everything and everyone.

In any difficult or stressful situation ask the three empowering questions:

What is great? Or, what could be great?

What's not perfect yet?

What can I do to remedy the situation and have fun in the process?

Gratitude is the seed of Abundant Happiness. From now on I will find things to be grateful for.

It is only my thoughts that make me feel happy or unhappy, not my circumstances. I control my thoughts, therefore I control my happiness.

The
POWER
of the
BODY

The second person on the young man's list was a man by the name of Rodney Greenway. Mr. Greenway was a well-known fitness instructor; not only did he own one of the leading health clubs in the city, but he had also written several books on health and fitness which had become international best-sellers.

The young man arrived at Mr. Greenway's health club promptly at the arranged time of 8 A.M. and was met by a tall, muscular, clean-cut man casually dressed in blue denim jeans and a white T-shirt. Mr. Greenway certainly looked the part with a slightly tanned complexion, short, dark-brown hair, and bright green eyes that seemed to glow when he smiled.

Mr. Greenway led the young man into his office and they both sat down on the easy chairs.

"Would you like something to eat or drink?" Mr. Greenway asked the young man. "We've got fruit juice, mineral water, herb teas . . . "

"A fruit juice would be great. Thank you," said the young man. Mr. Greenway poured out two glasses of fresh apple juice and handed one to the young man.

"So how can I help you?" he asked.

"I'm not sure," said the young man, and he proceeded to tell his story.

"The secrets of Abundant Happiness!" said Mr. Greenway. "I came across them over 10 years ago. In those days I was still working as a lawyer."

"A lawyer?" repeated the young man. "You gave up a career in law to become a fitness instructor?"

"Yes, absolutely."

"But why? How could you give up something that you must have studied for, for many years, and which would have provided a lucrative career for the rest of your life?"

"Very simple," said Mr. Greenway. "I was unhappy. When I was a student, I really had no idea what I wanted to do with my life and the law seemed like a sensible option. I reasoned that even if, once qualified, I didn't like it, it would be an excellent stepping stone to other careers."

"But not to becoming a physical fitness instructor?"

"No. That's true. I became a fitness instructor because that is what I wanted to do. I did fairly well as a lawyer for a few years but my heart just wasn't in it. I became more and more tired and depressed as time went by. I even reached the stage when I found it difficult to get out of bed in the morning."

"I know the feeling well," said the young man.

"Then one day I had to stay late at the office and the caretaker came in. He could see something was wrong. I had my head in my hands, rubbing my eyeballs. I told him I was okay, just feeling a bit down. Then he asked me if I wanted to feel 'high.' I said, 'No thank you.' I didn't take drugs. 'What makes you think I was talking about drugs?' he said. I was intrigued; I couldn't imagine what else, other than drugs, could make you feel high."

The young man took out his pen and notebook from his pocket and began to scribble notes.

"And do you know what the caretaker said? 'Exercise!'"

"Exercise?" exclaimed the young man, looking up from his notebook.

"Yes. Simple physical exercise."

"How on earth can exercise make you feel high?" asked the young man.

"Physical exercise isn't just necessary for physical health, it is also necessary to maintain long-term mental and emotional health, and there are sound reasons for this.

"You may have noticed that the advice people most often give to someone who is feeling a little depressed is to do something. It's good advice too, I use the acronym, G-O-Y-A."

"What does that stand for?" asked the young man.

"Get Off Your . . . Backside!"

The young man smiled as he wrote it down.

"The reason why it's good advice is that it works. As George Bernard Shaw once wrote: 'The secret of being miserable is to have the leisure to think about whether you are happy or not.' But, getting up and doing something doesn't just help take our mind off our problems; it changes our perceptions of those problems and relieves the stress that the problems create."

"How can exercise change the way we feel?" asked the young man in disbelief.

"I will have trouble telling you anything which is more important than this today: Motion affects emotion!"

The young man wrote it down.

"When we move our bodies, we change our emotional states. It is well known that people who don't exercise regularly develop muscle atrophy, physical weakness, calcium loss from their bones, and are more than twice as likely to die prematurely than people who do exercise regularly. But, what is not as well known is that people who do not exercise regularly also tend to become introverted, tense, and oversensitive as well as suffer more from depression, anxiety, and mental fatigue."

"Why is that?" asked the young man.

"Scientists discovered that there is a very good explanation for this phenomenon. They found that exercise causes the brain to release certain chemicals and hormones—endorphins and encephalines. These are natural stimulants which make you feel enervated or 'high'."

"Are you saying that we will feel happier if we exercise regularly?" asked the young man.

"Absolutely," replied Mr. Greenway.

"What sort of exercise?"

"'Aerobic' exercise. Now before you ask, that does not necessarily mean you should do a Jane Fonda workout," said Mr. Greenway smiling. "'Aerobic' literally means 'exercising with oxygen' and therefore includes any activity or sport in which you breathe as you do the exercise such as swimming, cycling, brisk walking, even dancing. Non-aerobic exercise, on the other hand, involves exercising without using oxygen and includes those activities in which you hold your breath such as sprinting and weightlifting, and is not as good for your emotions or your health."

"Why is that?" The young man was curious.

"Because when you do non-aerobic exercise, instead of burning oxygen, your body will burn glycogen which is food for the brain."

"How much exercise do you need to do to start to notice the benefits?" asked the young man.

"Only about 30 minutes or so every day. That's all."

"That doesn't sound too difficult," said the young man.

"It's not," replied Mr. Greenway, "although, like any change to your lifestyle, it does require determination to do it regularly and make it become a habit."

"So you're saying exercise can help you feel happier?"

"Yes. I had my doubts too," said Mr. Greenway, seeing that the young man was not convinced. "I had a long talk with the caretaker in my office that evening. He mentioned the 10 secrets of Abundant Happiness, and I must say that they all radically changed my life. But the one secret which I think I most needed to learn and the one which I am now most qualified to help you with is . . . the power of your body."

"By 'body' I assume you mean exercise," said the young man.

"No. There are a number of other equally important aspects about the way in which we use our bodies which also have a profound and immediate effect on our emotions of which exercise is only one."

The young man was fascinated and wrote notes as Mr. Greenway continued.

"The first thing is our posture—the way we stand, sit, and walk. If our posture is poor (i.e. bent over or leaning to one side instead of being straight and erect) our health and emotions suffer."

"I find that hard to believe. How can the way we stand or sit possibly affect our emotions?" asked the young man.

"Let me explain," said Mr. Greenway. "Imagine that outside this room, there is a man who is feeling lethargic, tired, and depressed. How do you think he will be sitting or standing?"

"I'm not sure."

"Well, would he be holding his head erect or would his head be slumped and facing the floor?"

"Facing the floor."

"Would his chest be pushed out or slouched?"

"Slouched, I suppose."

"Would his facial muscles be pulled up, tight and smiling, or would the muscles be flaccid and frowning?"

"Well, it's hardly likely they would be smiling," said the young man.

"And would he be breathing deeply or shallowly?"

"Shallowly. Okay, I get the picture," said the young man. "We adopt different postures according to the emotions we are feeling."

"Exactly. But it's a two-way street—our emotions affect our posture, but our posture also affects our emotions. If we slouch and hunch over all the time, we will begin to feel depressed, whereas if we stand erect we immediately feel better. It sounds incredible, doesn't it, but by changing our posture we can instantly change our emotional state. Did you know, for instance, that if you stand erect, breathe deeply, and smile, it is virtually impossible to feel depressed. Researchers have even taken people who are manic depressives—some who have been on medication for over 20 years—and monitored how they felt in different postures. The scientists were amazed to find that while they were standing like this, none of the patients felt depressed or needed medication. Can you imagine that?"

"But, surely you're not suggesting that the answer to everyone's problems is to spend more time standing erect, breathing deeply and smiling?"

"No, of course not. But it's a great start. It does help us to feel better and it works instantly. It's simply a way in which we can take control of our emotional states using our bodies.

"One of the secrets of being happy is being aware of your posture. We often develop bad posture through continued misuse—sitting hunched over a desk at work or slouched in front of the TV, but this will make you feel depressed."

"But it is so uncomfortable standing erect," said the young man. "It's like being a soldier on parade."

"Good posture is not standing to attention. In fact, that's very poor posture because it creates so much additional tension in your back. A healthy posture is simply keeping your back straight and relaxed. You shouldn't feel any tightness or pain at all. One of the best techniques which helps improve your posture is what I call the 'rope technique'."

"Rope technique? Sounds interesting," said the young man.

"It's quite straightforward and very easy to do. All you do is imagine that there is a rope attached to the top of your head and that there is a man standing above you who is gently pulling the rope upward."

The young man tried doing it and immediately felt he was not only straighter but taller as well.

"When you do this, you feel like you are being gently lifted and straightened, don't you?" said Mr. Greenway. "And, as a result, you feel better.

"Another very powerful technique using your body to help change your feelings is called 'anchoring'."

"Anchoring?"

"Yes. It's very simple and extremely effective. It's a bit like Pavlov's dog. You might recall that every time Pavlov's dog was given food, a bell was rung. The dog subconsciously associated the sound of the bell with food, and eventually just the sound of the bell alone made the dog salivate. Pavlov's dog had subconsciously associated or anchored the sound of the bell with food. The same thing happens with humans. How do you feel when you hear a dentist's drill? Tense? Uncomfortable? It's the same thing, we associate the sound of the drill with pain, discomfort, and tension.

"Often we subconsciously create anchors that are not conducive to happiness. I'll give you an example; if two people continually argue, there will come a time when all they have to do is see each other or hear each others' voice and they become angry."

"I'm still not sure how this applies to being happy," said the young man.

"We have positive anchors as well. You must have seen sports men and women clenching their fists and shouting 'Yes!' to pump themselves up. It's because this makes us feel confident and energetic. Try it for yourself now and see."

"It's okay," said the young man, his face reddening. "I'll take your word for it."

"Don't take my word for it, try it," said Mr. Greenway. "Stand up, clench your fists, and shout 'YES!'"

The young man stood up, clenched his fists, and said, "Yes!"

"No. Don't just say it," said Mr. Greenway. "Shout it."

So the young man did it again, but this time shouting it aloud. And to his amazement, he instantly felt energized.

"That's amazing!" he said. "It really works."

"Of course it does. There's more as well," said Mr. Greenway. "You can create your own anchors to produce specific emotions. Let me show you. Think back to a time when you felt really happy," said Mr. Greenway. The young man had to go back 10 years to the time when he celebrated getting his first job offer.

"Think of it as clearly as you can. Close your eyes and try to re-experience it. What you were saying? What you were doing? How were you breathing? Try to notice everything," said Mr. Greenway. The young man pictured the scene and then he suddenly felt Mr.

Greenway touch on his right shoulder. "Now remember it again," Mr. Greenway said and once again, as the young man was visualizing the past experience, Mr. Greenway touched his right shoulder.

"What are you doing?" said the young man.

"Don't worry. We need to do it a few more times and then I'll explain."

So the same process was repeated seven more times before the young man said, "What's this all about?"

"I have just created a 'happy' anchor for you," smiled Mr. Greenway.

"I don't understand . . . " the young man said, but just then Mr. Greenway touched him on his right shoulder and, to the young man's amazement, and for no apparent reason, he suddenly felt happy.

"I helped your subconscious associate happiness with being touched on the right shoulder," explained Mr. Greenway. "You see, it's that simple to create a feeling of happiness using an 'anchor'! All you need to do is: remember a time when you felt happy, really very happy and then, in the peak of the emotion as you are remembering it, do something unusual— pinch your ear, tweak your nose, squeeze your wrist. It doesn't matter what you do so long as it's specific and not something you do every day."

"Why's that?" interrupted the young man.

"Well, it's like Pavlov's dog again, if it heard the bell all day long, it wouldn't have associated it with the food. The wonderful thing is that you can use anchors to trigger any kind of emotional state—confidence, affection, compassion—literally any emotion."

"That sounds incredible," said the young man.

"So, for instance, if I want to feel confident, all I have to do is remember a time when I felt confident, do a specific action like pulling my earlobe whilst I'm remembering it, and if I do it over and over again, eventually all I will have to do to feel confident is pull my earlobe?"

"Precisely. It can take time to practice visualizing a past experience and remembering a specific memory, and you must be in the peak of the emotion before you create the anchor, but if you persevere, you'll see how easily it works."

"It sounds a bit simplistic," said the young man.

"I know, but it really does work. In fact, it works so well that advertisers use 'anchors' all the time to get you to associate good feelings with their products."

"How do they do that?" asked the young man. "Advertisers can't touch you."

"Anchors can be created through any of the senses—touch, sound, taste, smell, or sight. Pavlov's dog was anchored using the sound of a bell, and remember the example I gave you earlier of two people arguing who eventually would become angry just by seeing or hearing the other?"

"Yes. I see what you mean," said the young man.

"What advertisers commonly do is take one of the top pop stars and play his or her music whilst advertising a product. People feel good when they hear the music or see the pop star and pretty soon that feeling becomes anchored to the product. Why do you think a major soft drinks manufacturer paid Michael Jackson over $15 million to use him and his music in their adverts?

"Advertisers use anchors all the time, and we can

use them in just the same way, but for our own needs instead of theirs. This is the power of your body. But, that's not all. There are other very important ways in which our bodies affect our emotions. Food for instance."

"How does food come into all this?" said the young man.

"The food we put into our bodies influences the way we feel. For instance, processed sugary foods such as white bread, cakes, and chocolates all affect your blood sugar level and can make you feel tired and irritable, and excess coffee and tea and alcohol are known to contain stimulants that can cause depressed feelings. Some common artificial food additives have also been shown to cause depression. Research studies have, for instance, revealed that aspartame, one of the most common artificial sweeteners used in many 'sugar-free' drinks and foods throughout the world, may actually cause clinical depression in some people."

"Are there any foods that help you feel good?" enquired the young man.

"Well, medical studies have revealed that rutin, a bioflavinoid found in buckwheat, has a beneficial effect on our brain waves and can help 'lift' people out of depression. But, basically, it is important to have a nutritious whole food diet with lots of fresh fruits and vegetables and whole grains (such as brown rice, oats, barley, millet, and whole wheat bread and pasta) because this will help regulate blood sugar levels, reduce irritability, and help counter the effects of stress."

The young man thought about all the ready-made

meals he was used to having. There was no way that there was much freshness in TV dinners. Perhaps this had also been a contributing factor to his general lethargy and unhappiness.

"But one of the most neglected areas in emotional well-being," continued Mr. Greenway, "in relation to our bodily needs is natural daylight."

"Natural daylight?" repeated the young man as he scribbled down his notes. "Well, we all get that, don't we?"

"Unfortunately, we often don't. Many people work in factories or offices that have no windows, or windows that are tinted to block out the sunlight. It's a lot worse in the winter of course when the days are so much shorter. In fact, depression caused by lack of daylight is now an established medical disorder— Seasonal Affective Disorder or SAD for short. That is why there are so many more suicides recorded in winter months."

"So what we can do about it?"

"Either get out in the daylight for at least an hour a day or, if that is not possible, use natural daylight bulbs."

"This has been absolutely fascinating," said the young man. "I never realized how important our bodies are to the way we feel. Why aren't people made aware of all of this?"

"That is why they are called 'secrets'," said Mr. Greenway. "I think, deep down, we all 'know' how to use our bodies and how to be happy—it's the most natural state in the world—it's just that living in the modern world, we have forgotten and sometimes we need to be reminded.

"After I first learned all of this, I started to try and incorporate it into my daily routines. I went for a brisk walk every morning before work, I was conscious of my posture, I started eating sensibly with plenty of fresh fruits and vegetables, pulses, pasta, rice, and potatoes, and I tried to spend an hour every day out in the daylight.

"The results were incredible. After one week, I was so amazed by the difference in the way I felt that I decided to devote my life to sharing this with others. I trained in physiotherapy and personal fitness and to begin with I worked some evenings and at the weekend. Within a few months my business had taken off so well that I was able to do it full time. It's incredible how much better you feel when you really believe in and enjoy your work. In fact, I wouldn't call it work at all. It's fun."

"And it was all thanks to your office caretaker," said the young man.

"Yes, it was. I tried to contact him a few weeks later to thank him for his help, but nobody had ever heard of him."

"Hold on," said the young man. "He was . . . an old Chinese man?"

Mr. Greenway smiled. "Who else?"

When the young man arrived home he sat down and read his notes.

The second secret of Abundant Happiness—the power of your body.

Motion affects emotion.

Exercise relieves stress and causes a chemical reaction making us feel good. Exercise regularly—daily if possible—for a minimum of 30 minutes.

My feelings are influenced by my posture. A strong posture creates a happy disposition.

The feeling of happiness can be consciously triggered at any time using an "anchor."

The foods we eat influence the way we feel. Avoid depressants such as coffee, tea, alcohol, sugary foods, and artificial additives. Have plenty of fresh fruits and vegetables, whole grains, and pulses.

Lack of natural daylight can cause feelings of depression. Get out in the daylight for an hour a day, if possible.

The
POWER
of the
MOMENT

"It happened almost 20 years ago. Things weren't going well at work and I was having problems at home as well. Then one day I was walking briskly up the main street in the center of town at about four in the afternoon, on my way to give a presentation to one of our major clients. Suddenly, I heard a horn blowing and a woman scream. I looked up and saw a huge juggernaut heading straight at me.

"Everything seemed to happen in slow motion. I just stood there, paralyzed by fear as the juggernaut skidded toward me. I thought that was it, I was going to die, but at the last second, I felt someone grab me and pull me backward. It was a close thing, I can tell you. I actually felt the side of the juggernaut skim past my overcoat. Another centimeter and I would have been hit and doubtless killed. I turned around to see who it was who had saved my life and there he was, a little old Chinese man!"

Tony Brown was in his mid-forties. He was a successful freelance photographer whose photographs regularly appeared in the national newspapers and magazines. The young man had met Mr. Brown at his studio in the center of the town.

"I was a little shaken by the incident and sat down on a nearby bench," continued Mr. Brown. "The old Chinese man came and sat down next to me, and asked if I was all right. I told him that I'd be fine. 'That was close,' he said. 'I know. Thank you,' I said. 'You saved my life.' I explained that my mind had been elsewhere when I had stepped out into the road, and then he said something that made me think. He said: 'There is a saying in my country: the only place to live is here, the only time to live is now!'

"We talked; only for a few minutes, but just before he left, he handed me a piece of paper."

"And it contained a list of 10 names and phone numbers?" interrupted the young man.

"Yes," replied Mr. Brown with a smile. "This is how I learned the secrets of Abundant Happiness."

"What did they do for you?" asked the young man.

"They taught me how to create happiness. And one in particular left a very deep impression on me, probably because it was something I had never considered . . . the power of living in the moment."

"How can a moment contain any power or secret of happiness?" asked the young man.

"The secret is not in the moment, it is *living in the moment*," said Mr. Brown. "Happiness cannot be found in years, months, weeks, or even days—it is found only by living in the moment."

"What do you mean?" asked the young man, still confused. "You're not saying that you cannot be happy for more than a minute, are you?"

"Of course not. But I am saying that you can only experience happiness moment by moment. Look at these pictures over here," said Mr. Brown. "What do you see?"

The young man studied the photographs on the wall next to him. Each frame captured an expression. There was a young mother cradling her baby; a father and son laughing, playing ball; two elderly men hugging; two friends in an airport crying, and a crowd of children playing in a school playground.

Finally, he said, "Well, there's a lot of intense emotions and feeling. They're very good."

"Thank you," said Mr. Brown, "It's the emotions I try to capture. This is the beauty of photographs, they record one split second of time—a split second that will never be repeated again—in which we experience an emotion. Have you ever thought about how people place value on things such as television sets, computers, cars, money, clothes, jewelry . . . all things that can easily be replaced. But, time is the one thing in life that can never be replaced and yet we think of it as having no value. It is the most valuable resource we have and yet we tend to squander it. Thinking about the past or worrying about the future deprives us of the present. And the present—the here and now—is all we have, and all we can ever have."

"I'm not sure I understand," said the young man.

"When you look back on your life," explained Mr.

Brown, "and remember happy times what comes to mind?"

"Let me think . . . " said the young man looking away. He thought of his fifth birthday when his father had still been alive, and then there were the family holidays by the sea, graduation from college . . .

"How do you remember those times?" asked Mr. Brown. "As years or months or weeks or days . . . or moments?"

"I'm not sure," said the young man.

"Well, think of one that really stands out."

"Okay, my fifth birthday party."

"When exactly did you feel happy?"

"Just before the party began, I remember my mother hugged me and whispered: 'You are my special boy and I love you!' Sometimes, when I close my eyes, I can still hear her saying it in my ear."

"Excellent!" said Mr. Brown, pleased to be able to prove his point. "You see that was a moment! All children live in the moment. Imagine what would have happened if, at the time, you had been thinking about school work? You may not have heard what your mother had said and you would have missed the feeling of happiness. Your mother would have also missed out on the happiness that your reaction no doubt gave her."

"I see what you mean," said the young man.

"All of our memories are made up of moments—moments when we saw, heard, or felt something. We don't remember years or months or even days—only moments. We can therefore only get the most out of life by getting the most of each moment. If a moment is special, magical, then life becomes special and magical. The secret is to collect as many of those moments as you can. There will never be another now, so the best we can do is make the most of it. Always remember that, whilst life at this moment may not be all you want, at this moment it's all you have. 'So,' as one wise man once said, 'why not stick a flower in your buttonhole and be happy?'"

The young man remembered the story he had been told by Mr. Kesterman of the man who, despite being terminally ill, remained cheerful because he was grateful for each day he lived. The dying man must have learned the power of living in the moment. Living moment by moment, day by day, he had been able to be happy in spite of his illness.

"There is a saying," continued Mr. Brown. "'Living yard by yard, life is hard. But inch by inch, life's a cinch!' Everything is easy when it's broken down into small pieces. If you live in the moment you have no time for regrets and no time for worries, you only have what lies before you."

But the young man was still confused. "How do you get the most out of a moment?" he asked.

"By being aware," replied Mr. Brown. "Dante said, 'Think that this day will never dawn again!'

"If you're not aware that someone is offering you an apple, you won't take it. It's a bit like a highly ranked tennis player in a big championship tournament who, in an opening round against an unranked player, thinks about the opponent he will have to play in the final and, as a result, makes an unforced error which loses him a point. He plays the shot over in his mind, and is unable to concentrate on the next shot. Consequently, he makes another error. Again he chastises himself for the needlessly lost points and becomes anxious: 'What if I lose the match?' Needless to say, worrying about something which has not yet happened also prevents him from concentrating on the present shot, and he loses yet another point. Before he knows it, it is all over—game, set, and match.

"The same thing happens in our lives. We mull over the past and worry about the future and, consequently, we never give the present our full attention. This leads to feelings of regret for things done and anxiety over things which haven't happened. If you do not live in the moment you cannot win the game of Life."

The young man raised an eyebrow. It seemed so obvious and yet he had never really thought about the significance of time in this way.

"If we are to be happy," continued Mr. Brown, "we must learn to appreciate what we have, and all we have is here and now. Today's decisions are tomorrow's realities. We must learn to take things as they come and to let them go as they depart. As Thomas Carlyle wrote: 'Our main business is not to see what lies dimly at a distance, but to do what lies clearly at hand.' If we focus on the distant future we can become overwhelmed and depressed. Many people spend their time worrying about things which have never and probably will never happen. Montaigne, the French philosopher, wrote: 'My life has been full of terrible misfortunes ... most of which never happened.' This is one of the reasons why so many people are burdened by worry and stress—for them, today is the tomorrow they worried about yesterday!

Living in the moment leaves no room for regret over the past or anxiety about the future. Instead of facing what is ahead of you or behind you, you focus only on what is in front of you.

"This is why to live in the moment—to take one moment at a time—is one of the best ways to overcome worry and fear.

Most religions adopt this philosophy. When Jesus was asked how a person should pray, he recited in the Lord's prayer: 'Give us *this* day our daily bread.' Not tomorrow's bread or next week's or next year's, only today's. One way people manage to survive personal tragedies in their lives is by taking one day at a time, and if that philosophy can get us through the worst times, imagine how much better it can make the good times! This is why it is written that, to a wise man, each day is a new beginning. I keep this," he said, handing the young man a plaque from the wall, "and read it every day to remind myself of that wisdom and to make sure I live in the moment. It helps me make the best of each day and therefore the best of my life."

The plaque was inscribed with the prose of an Indian poet entitled: *Salutation to the Dawn:*

Look to this day!
For it is life, the very life of life.
In its brief course
Lie all the verities and realities of your existence:
The bliss of growth
The glory of action
The splendor of beauty

For yesterday is but a dream
And tomorrow is only a vision
But today well lived makes every yesterday a
dream of happiness
And every tomorrow a vision of hope.

Look well, therefore, to this day! Such is the
salutation of the dawn.

Kalidasa

"Try it for yourself," said Mr. Brown. "For the rest
of the day focus your mind only on what you are
doing instead of what you have done or what you
will be doing."

"I think I understand," said the young man. "But
what about concern for the future?"

"It is only by living in the moment that we can create the future that we desire. Every moment offers us
choices which will shape our destiny. Thought is the
seed of action, action creates a habit, habits mold
character, and our character creates our destiny.

"The thoughts that we choose in any one moment
determine where we will be in the next. This is why
the decisions and actions we take in any moment create our future. When you talk to people, you will soon
find that all too often they are living in the past or
future, in other times and places, instead of making
the best of what they have here and now. This is precisely what happened to me, and the fact that I was
often thinking about things other than the matter at
hand nearly got me killed. If you don't live in the
moment, you might not get run over by a truck, but

you'll miss most of the experiences and opportunities that come your way."

"So, you're not suggesting that people should not plan ahead, are you?" asked the young man.

"Not at all. Planning is vital before we take any action. But don't plan something when you're doing something else and don't do something else when you're planning something. Whatever you are thinking or doing, focus on that activity, one thing at a time. When you are talking to someone give them your full attention; when you're working, focus your mind on the job at hand, and don't make the same mistake I did."

"What was that?" asked the young man.

"When you cross the road, be aware of the traffic! Once you live in the moment you reduce feelings of anxiety and depression, improve your performance at work, enhance your personal relationships, and generally enrich your life. This is the power of living in the moment."

For the rest of that day, the young man tried to keep his mind attentive to what he was doing. It wasn't easy to stop his thoughts straying at times but generally he managed to concentrate on what he was doing and he was left in no doubt that he was better off for it. Instead of worrying about the backlog of paperwork on his desk, he tackled one letter at a time and for the first time since he joined the company three years ago, at the end of the day, the "to do" tray was empty. When he spoke to work colleagues he gave them his full attention and was surprised when one man said, "Thanks for listening. You were really helpful." And that made him feel good about himself.

Later that evening the young man sat down and examined the notes he had made in his meeting that day.

The third secret of Abundant Happiness—the power of living in the moment.

Happiness is found not in years or months or weeks or even days, but it can be found in each moment.

The
POWER
of
SELF-
IMAGE

It was not until the following week that the young man was able to meet the next person on his list. Ruth Moses explained that she would be away on a study trip for her degree course in Archaeology but she would gladly meet with him on her return.

When the young man arrived at Ruth Moses' apartment he was met by a fresh-faced elderly lady dressed in denim dungarees and a pink sweat shirt.

"Hello," he said, "I'm here to see Ruth Moses."

"Yes. Hello," said the lady smiling. "Please do come in."

The old lady led the young man into the lounge. "Make yourself comfortable," she said. "The kettle has just boiled. Would you like some tea? I've got Earl Grey, decaffeinated coffee, and a selection of herb teas—fruit, chamomile, peppermint, orange blossom."

"Peppermint tea would be nice. Thank you," answered the young man.

A few moments passed before the old lady returned carrying a tray with a pot of freshly-boiled water, two cups, an assortment of herb teas, a jar of honey, and a plate of homemade biscuits. She sat down opposite the young man and started pouring the tea.

"Now then," she said, "I was intrigued by your phone call. Tell me again what it's all about."

The young man looked perplexed. "I'm sorry . . . you're Ruth Moses?"

"Of course!" grinned the old lady. "Who did you think I was?"

"Erm . . . I . . . don't know . . . but I thought you said on the phone that you were a student?"

"I am. I'm currently doing a degree in Archaeology. God willing, next year I'll be doing a masters. Would you like some honey with your tea?"

"No, thank you."

She passed him a cup of tea and offered him some biscuits.

"Are you kidding me?" asked the young man.

"About what?"

"You really are an undergraduate?" persisted the young man.

Mrs. Moses smiled. "Yes, of course."

"Well . . . er . . . forgive me," said the young man, trying not to cause offense at his surprise. "It's just that, after we spoke on the phone, I expected you to be a young student."

"I am a young student," insisted Mrs. Moses with a mischievous grin. "Eighty-two years young to be precise!"

The young man smiled. "I can't argue with that," he said.

"So, how can I help you?" asked Mrs. Moses.

The young man proceeded to tell her about his meeting with the old Chinese man.

"Look at this," Mrs. Moses said handing the young man a photograph.

"Who is it?" asked the young man as he looked at the black-and-white photograph of an old, almost haggard lady with a walking stick. "Your mother?"

"No. It's me, or rather, it was me . . . 20 years ago."

The young man took a closer look at the photograph and whilst he could see a certain resemblance in the bone structure, the hairline and the shape of the mouth, there was very little else to suggest that the lady in the picture was the same lady who sat in front of him.

"It looks like you got younger rather than older since this picture was taken. What on earth happened? How did you do it?"

"I met someone who changed my life . . . an old Chinese man! Shortly after I retired 20 or so years ago, I started to feel old for the first time. I had difficulty getting to sleep at night but I was tired during the day. I began to lose my powers of concentration and memory, and my limbs were beginning to feel stiff and heavy. As you can imagine, I became pretty miserable, but then one day everything changed. I was waiting for a bus and standing beside me was an elderly Chinese man carrying a rucksack on his back.

"The old man smiled at me, so I smiled back and we began talking. He told me that he was traveling around the world. I couldn't believe it. How could a man his age have the strength and energy to travel around the world with a rucksack on his back? I asked him, of course, and he laughed. 'We are only as old as we think we are,' he said. We began talking about life after 60, and whilst I could only see problems and difficulties, he saw advantages and opportunities. 'With age comes experience and wisdom,' he said. And then he asked me something I had never considered before: Why should life be any less fulfilling just because you have lived longer? 'If anything,' he said, 'life should be better because you have had more practice at it!'

"Talking with the Chinese man that day made me realize for the first time the truth in the proverb 'A man is as he thinks in his heart.' What makes a person old is not their age but their mind. I enjoyed talking to the Chinese man so much that I let at least four buses pass by. I was captivated by the secrets of Abundant Happiness—secrets through which anyone—of any age, creed, or color—can create happiness in their lives. The secrets gave me a new lease of life. It was like being reborn. It was as if everything changed from being black and white into the most wonderful, bright colors. But, of course, nothing changed except me. And that turned out to be the value of the secrets for me . . . the power of our self-image."

"Self-image?" repeated the young man quizzically.

"Yes. How you see yourself, the beliefs you have about yourself. One of the reasons many people are so unhappy with their lives is simply that they are unhappy with themselves. Can you believe that deep down many people do not really like themselves? A lot of people grow up with complexes; sometimes physical, such as, 'My nose is too big' or 'I'm ugly' or 'too young' or 'too old'; sometimes the complexes are intellectual, such as, 'I'm not as clever as other people', and sometimes they believe they have a defective personality such as, 'I have no sense of humor' or 'I'm boring.' But whatever the reason, if you are not happy with yourself, how can you be happy with life?"

The young man immediately thought about his own complexes, and there were plenty of them. "Where do all these complexes come from?" he asked.

"Our life experiences. Usually from our childhood. I remember one man told me, 'I grew up to have my father's speech patterns, my father's posture, my father's opinions . . . and my mother's contempt for my father!'

"Our impressions of ourselves are, of course, first formed in infancy. We don't know who or what we are or what we should be, but we learn from those around us, those who are older and wiser and supposedly love us.

"Let me give you an example: little Jimmy comes home from school with a bad report card. He wonders to himself: 'Why have I done so badly? Maybe it's because I watch too much TV, maybe I haven't worked hard enough, maybe I'm stupid, or maybe I'm just lazy.' He hands his report card to his father. The father looks at the card, there are no As and Bs, only Ds and Es. He says to Jimmy, 'Well, one thing's obvious—you haven't been cheating!' But as he studies the report in more detail and reads the teachers' comments about his son, Jimmy's father becomes angry. He says: 'The problem with you, Jimmy, is you don't work hard enough, you're lazy and stupid!'

"Now Jimmy has no more doubts about himself, he *knows* that he is lazy and stupid and he carries this knowledge throughout his entire life. Every time he sees a challenge he says to himself, 'I can't do that because I'm stupid and lazy.' So he avoids challenges, he sees himself as inferior to others, and he resents being himself."

"So, how can we get rid of these complexes or negative beliefs?" asked the young man.

"That's a good question. The first thing we need to do is ask ourselves one of the most important questions we can ever ask: 'Who or what am I?'"

"Why?"

"Because the answer will help us appreciate how special we all are. For instance, did you know that, even after your mother and father met and mated, the chances of you being born were less than one in 300,000 billion! There could have been 300,000 billion other completely different people born in your place, but you made it. Not only that, but there has never been a person exactly like you in the history of the world, and neither will there ever be anyone exactly like you.

"The next question we need to ask is, 'What are my beliefs about myself?'"

"What, such as, 'I'm ugly or stupid'?" interrupted the young man.

"Yes. And then consider, 'How do I know for certain that it's true?' Was it because of what someone else said or did, or do you know it for a fact to be true? You see, most of the time we develop our beliefs about ourselves from other people. People are sort of like psychological mirrors of us. But let me show you something."

Mrs. Moses pulled out some mirrors from her desk drawer. She held each mirror up for the young man to look at himself. They were all curved and distorted mirrors, miniatures of those which are often seen at a funfair, and the young man hardly recognized himself. One made his head look a meter long, another made his ears look like wings, and another made him look like the fattest man on earth. The young man laughed at his reflections.

"Which one looks like you?" asked Mrs. Moses.

"None of them," replied the young man.

"How do you know?"

"Because they're 'play' mirrors. They can't give a true reflection."

"Of course. But what would have happened if you had never seen a true reflection of yourself? You might have been horrified when you looked in these play mirrors. Fortunately, you know what you look like physically because you have seen yourself before in a proper, unbiased mirror. But when have you ever seen a true, unbiased image of what you look like psychologically? You see, whilst we have mirrors which reveal what we look like physically, we don't have mirrors which show us what we look like psychologically. Instead, we rely on the reactions of other people to find out who we are on the inside. If people say you are selfish, you may believe that you are selfish. Similarly, if someone tells you that you're stupid, you might believe that too. People are mirrors of us, yes, but they are distorted mirrors—they carry their own prejudices which distort their image of you.

"The biggest mistake you can make in your life is to rely on other people to find out who you really are. When a parent or teacher says to a child, 'You *are* naughty' or 'You *are* selfish' or 'lazy' or 'stupid', they are creating a negative—and false—self-image for the child. True, the child may have done or said something which was naughty, selfish, lazy, or stupid, but that was the child's behavior, not the child. It's a subtle difference, but an important one. It's the difference between saying, 'You are a naughty girl' and "It's naughty to throw juice over the carpet.'"

"Isn't it the same thing, really?" asked the young man.

"Have you ever done something that you later regretted? Made a silly mistake or done something stupid?"

The young man nodded. "Hasn't everybody?"

"Now, just because you made a stupid mistake, does it mean that you are a stupid person?"

"I see what you mean," said the young man.

"Many people confuse the behavior with the person, and as a result we develop negative beliefs about ourselves which are not necessarily true, but which we carry with us throughout our lives."

The young man scribbled some notes on his pad. "I understand how we can develop negative beliefs or complexes about ourselves," he said. "But, once we have developed them, how can we get rid of them?"

"Well, being able to identify where the belief came from is the first step," said Mrs. Moses. "Sometimes an awareness is all it takes to eliminate the problem.

However, there are some beliefs which are so deeply rooted in our psyche that their eradication requires more than an awareness of their origins. In these cases, one solution lies in 'positive affirmations'."

"What are 'affirmations'?" asked the young man.

"An affirmation is a statement we say to ourselves, either aloud or in our head. A positive affirmation might therefore be something like: 'I am a loving, intelligent, unique human being.'"

"Why should that help?" asked the young man.

"If we hear something often enough," explained Mrs. Moses, "we start to believe it. That is, after all, where most of our beliefs come from—hearing something over and over as a child. Advertisers use this technique all the time. They create a phrase and have it repeated over and over again in the media and eventually we all believe it.

"To take control of your life, you must take control of your beliefs, and using affirmations is one way of doing that."

"How often do you need to say a particular affirmation before your subconscious starts to believe it?" asked the young man.

"That of course depends upon how long you have had the opposite negative belief and how frequently you repeat the affirmation. It also helps if you say the affirmation with feeling, as if you really believe it rather than in an uncommitted, monotone voice. I would say try and repeat an affirmation at least three times a day—morning, noon, and evening. Write it on a card, if you like, and read it whenever you get a chance.

"Another technique which can help you change

your self-image is to act as if you were the opposite of your complex. For instance, if you believe that you're unattractive, act as if you are attractive, or if you think you lack confidence, act as if you were confident."

"Isn't that just pretending to be something that you're not?" said the young man.

"Yes. But an incredible thing happens when you act as if you're attractive, confident, and happy . . . you start to feel attractive, confident, and happy. Perhaps I can explain it better by example. Imagine a young girl who thinks she is unattractive going to a dance with her friends. All night long she stands in the corner where no one can see her and hardly surprisingly no one asks her to dance. Now if that same girl acted as if she was attractive, she might wear a more flattering dress, she might mingle more with people. She would relax and enjoy herself and in doing so would actually become more attractive to others.

"Or imagine a man about to give a speech. He is so nervous, his knees are shaking. If he acted the way he feels, he would turn around and run straight for the exit. But, he knows he must go through with it and so he tries to act as if he was confident. After a confident-sounding opening sentence, the audience applaud, and now he starts to feel confident. Likewise, sometimes we may not feel happy, but if we act is if we are happy and smile at people, more often than not, they will smile back and you perk up inside.

"Another way to improve our self-image is to search for things we like about ourselves."

"That sounds good in theory, but how easy is it to do in practice?" said the young man as he jotted down notes.

"Very easy," said Mrs. Moses. "All you need do is consciously ask yourself: 'What do I like about myself?' or 'What are the things I am good at?'"

"Yes, but the answer might be 'very little' or, even worse, 'nothing at all'," said the young man.

"One of the most wonderful things about the human mind is that it will always search for an answer to a question, and even if there is no answer it will often make one up. Most of the time, we ask negative questions—'Why am I unattractive?', 'Why am I so stupid?', 'Why can't I get a job?' Your brain will always find an answer to any question you ask of it about yourself—'Because you've got a big nose', 'Because you were born with a small brain', 'Because you're not as good as other people.' All nonsense, of course, but your brain found answers!

"When we ask positive questions we will likewise get positive answers. And, even if you have trouble thinking of something you like about yourself, rephrase the question: 'If there was something I liked about myself, what would it be?' This question forces a positive answer. Other excellent questions that will change the way we feel about ourselves are: 'What are my strengths?', 'What am I good at?', 'Where can I make an effective contribution?'

"Affirmations, acting as if, and asking positive questions are simple, effective ways through which we can start to change the way we feel about ourselves. We then need to stop taking on board false beliefs from the reactions of other people. We need to remember always that whilst people are our mirrors, they are prejudiced, inaccurate mirrors.

"If you remember one thing today, remember this: it

takes no talent, no brains, and no character to criticize. Only God can create a flower, but any foolish child can pull it to pieces! When people are hostile or rude, when they say cruel and unkind things, it is invariably a reflection of their own troubled spirit rather than a reflection of you. Therefore, don't listen to anybody who tries to tell you who or what you are (unless, of course, it is positive). If I listened to other people, do you think I would be studying at university at my age? If I accepted what other people used to say to me, do you think I would have learned to ski when I was 65? Or learned to paint when I was 68? If I listened to other people I'd probably be dead or living off memories by now.

"People said I was a fool to start all these things at my age. Many still think I'm a little mad. Perhaps I am, but I'll tell you one thing—I'm happy with my life.

"I once read that the highest thing you can attain in life is to know yourself because only then are you truly free—free of the limitations and restrictions that others may wish to impose upon you, and free to live as we were meant to live . . . being happy."

The young man felt inspired. "This sounds so simple and it makes so much sense, but . . . does it really work?"

Mrs. Moses smiled, "There is only one way to find out. Try it!"

That night, before going to bed, the young man read over the notes he had made that day.

The fourth secret of Abundant Happiness—the power of self-image.

It is written, "A man is as he thinks in his heart." We are what we think we are. If I am unhappy with myself, I will be unhappy with life. Therefore to be happy in life, I must first be happy with myself.

Every person is special. Every person is a winner because every person overcame odds of one in 300,000 billion when they were born.

People are mirrors of us, but they are distorted mirrors.

To overcome complexes and negative beliefs about myself, and create a positive self-image, I must:

First find out where they came from and whether they are true. (If they are true, resolve to change.)

Make positive affirmations every day affirming the type of person I wish to be.

Act as if I am the way I would like to be.

Ask myself what I do like or respect about myself.

The
POWER
of
GOALS

Two days later the young man met the fifth person on his list, Dr. Julius Franks. Dr. Franks was a professor in Psychology at the city university and although 70 years of age, he had a certain youthful vigor about him that transcended his years and reminded the young man of the old Chinese man.

"I met the old Chinese man many, many years ago," explained Dr. Franks. "I was in a prisoner-of-war camp in the Far East during the Second World War. The conditions were terrible, almost unbearable; meager rations of food, no clean water, and everywhere you looked there was dysentery, malaria, or sunstroke. Some of the prisoners couldn't cope with the physical and mental strain of the continuous heavy workloads in the hot sun and, for them, death became a welcome escape. I even thought about it myself, but one day someone restored my will to live—an old Chinese man."

The young man listened intently to Dr. Franks' account of what happened that day.

"I was sitting alone in the exercise yard feeling very weak and tired, and I was actually thinking about how easy it would be to run into the electrified boundary fence. The next thing I knew, an old Chinese man was sitting next to me. Even in my weakened state I was startled and thought I must be hallucinating. After all, how on earth could a Chinese man appear so suddenly and easily in a Japanese camp?

"He turned and asked me a question; a simple question that, quite literally, saved my life."

He paused for a moment.

The young man was perplexed. "How could a question save someone's life?" he thought.

"And that question was," continued Dr. Franks, "What is the first thing you are going to do when you get out of here?"

"It was something I had never even thought about, never dared to. But I knew the answer—I wanted to see my wife and children again. And, all of a sudden, I was reminded that I had something to live for, a reason why I would do everything I could to survive. That one question saved my life because it gave me something I had lost—a reason to live!

"Right then and there, the struggle to survive became an easier burden because I knew that each day I survived brought me closer to the end of the war and therefore closer to my dreams. The Chinese man's question not only saved my life, it taught me one of the most important lessons I have ever learned."

"What was that?" asked the young man.

"The power of goals."

"Goals?" repeated the young man.

"Yes. Goals. Ambitions. Things to strive for. Goals give our lives purpose and meaning. True, we can exist without them, but to really live, and live happily, we need our lives to have purpose. 'Without purpose,' wrote the great Admiral Byrd, 'the days would have ended, as such days always end, in disintegration.'"

"Disintegration of what?" asked the young man.

"The soul. Have you ever wondered why so many people lose their health and die so quickly after they retire? Have you ever wondered why so many rich and famous people end up as drug addicts or alcoholics?"

The young man nodded. He had often wondered why people became "old" once they retired and he had always been curious about why a famous celebrity, someone who seemed to have it all—a magnificent home or homes, more money than they could ever possibly spend in their lifetime, a family, a fabulous career—so often took to drugs or alcohol, or even committed suicide.

"One of the reasons," explained Dr. Franks, "is simply that they feel their lives have no purpose. Their lives have no meaning to them. Have you ever heard of Helen Keller?"

"Yes. Just last week as a matter a fact. I was told that, despite being blind, deaf, and dumb, she loved her life."

"Yes. And do you know why she loved it?" asked Dr. Franks. "Because she gave her life meaning. When she was asked how she managed to be so happy despite her handicaps, she answered: 'Many people have the wrong idea of what constitutes happiness. It is not attained through self-gratification, but through fidelity to a worthy purpose.' The most basic requirement the human soul craves is the need for meaning in life, and that is what goals give us.

"Goals create purpose and meaning. With goals, we know where we are going, we are driven toward something. Without goals, life has little meaning and we tend to drift aimlessly. It is because people are motivated by only one of two things—pain or pleasure. Goals focus the mind on pleasure, whereas lack of goals allows the mind to focus on avoiding pain. Goals can even make pain more bearable."

"I'm not sure I understand," said the young man. "How can goals make pain more bearable?"

"Let me see . . . yes, imagine a terrible abdominal pain. An intermittent sharp pain every few minutes. It's so excruciating that it's causing you to scream. How would you feel?"

"Pretty awful, I would imagine."

"How would you feel if the pain was getting worse and becoming more frequent? Would you be anxious or excited?"

"What sort of question is that? How can you be excited about pain? You'd have to be a masochist."

"No. You have to be a pregnant woman! She bears the pain but she knows that, at the end of it, she will have a baby. She may even look forward to the pains becoming more frequent because she knows that each contraction brings her closer to the birth of her child as well as to the end of the pain. The purpose or meaning behind the pain makes it more bearable.

"It is the same reason why living through hard times is made more bearable when we have something to look forward to at the end of it. There is no doubt that having goals to live for gave me the strength to survive when otherwise I would almost certainly have ended my life. Whenever I saw a fellow prisoner looking despondent I would ask him the same question: "What is the first thing you are going to do when you get out of here?" and gradually his face would change, a small light would shine in his eyes as the realization dawned upon him that he had things to live for. He had a future to strive for and he would do his very best to survive each day knowing that he was a little closer to his goal. And I'll tell you something else: seeing a man change so dramatically, and knowing that you played a small part in helping him is a wonderful feeling. So I made it my goal every day to help as many people as I could.

"One of the secrets of surviving the worst periods in our lives is the same as the secret of living life to the full in the best times. And that secret is—goals. If goals can give people in a prisoner-of-war camp the will to survive, what do you imagine they could do for people in peacetime?

"After the war, I became involved in a very interesting study at Harvard University. We asked the whole of the graduating year in 1953 if they had any ambitions or goals for their lives. How many of them do you think had specific goals?"

"Fifty percent?" guessed the young man.

"Less than three percent!" said Dr. Franks. "Can you imagine, less than three people in every hundred had any idea what they wanted to do with their lives!

"We followed their careers over the next 25 years and discovered that those three percent of undergraduates who had had goals had more stable marriages and better health, and were worth more financially than the other 97 percent put together. It was therefore no surprise to discover that they also had led far, far happier lives."

"Why do you think having goals makes people feel happier?" asked the young man.

"Because we get energy not just from food but from enthusiasm, and enthusiasm is produced by having goals, things to aim for, things to look forward to. One of the biggest reasons why so many people are unhappy is simply that they feel their lives have no meaning, no purpose. They have nothing to get out of bed in the morning for, they have no goals to inspire them, no dreams. They drift aimlessly through life with no direction.

"If we have something to aim for," continued Dr. Franks, "the stresses and strains of life seem to disappear. They are seen only as hurdles which must be overcome to reach that goal. This is why I advise all of my patients to learn the rocking-chair technique."

"What's that?" asked the young man.

"It's a simple technique in which you imagine you have lived your life and are now sitting in a rocking chair thinking back over how you lived and what you achieved. What would you want to be remembering? What things would you like to have done? What places would you like to have visited? What relationships would you like to have built? And, most importantly, as you sit there in the rocking chair, what type of person would you like to have become?"

The young made a few notes. These were powerful questions that he had never thought of asking himself before.

"This technique helps you create long-term goals. We then do the same thing with shorter-term goals— ten-year and five-year goals, one-year goals, six-month goals, one-month goals, and even daily goals. I then advise my patients to write down all of these goals and read them through first thing in the morning. That way, you always have something positive to get out of bed for in the morning and start the day enthused and excited."

"I'll try that," said the young man. "I always have difficulty getting out of bed in the morning."

"It's also a good idea to read through your goals sometime during the day and last thing at night to keep them impressed on your mind."

"What happens if my views change and I decide that I no longer want one of my goals?" asked the young man.

"That's a good question. Our priorities and values in life do change as we grow and we simply change our goals accordingly. This is why the rocking-chair technique should be done regularly—at least every year. That way we always have goals that we are committed to, which create purpose and meaning in our lives, things that excite and motivate us.

"Goals lay the foundation of our happiness. People often think that comfort and luxury are the chief requirements of happiness, but all we really need to feel happy is something to be enthusiastic about. This is one of the greatest secrets of Abundant Happiness—there is no lasting happiness in a life which is devoid of meaning and purpose. This is the power of goals."

"Did you ever meet the old Chinese man again?" asked the young man.

"No. In fact, for some time I was convinced that he was an hallucination or figment of my imagination."

"Why?"

"Because I had never seen him before and I never saw him again. Sometimes the hot sun can play tricks with your mind. But not long after the war, I found out that he really did exist."

"How?" asked the young man.

"I received a letter from a young man. A young man who had been given my name by an old Chinese man!"

Later in the day the young man summarized the notes he had made during his meeting.

The fifth secret of Abundant Happiness—the power of goals.

Goals give our lives purpose and meaning.

With goals, we focus on gaining pleasure rather than avoiding pain.

Goals give reasons to get out of bed in the morning.

Goals make difficult periods easier, and good times even better.

The rocking-chair technique helps you to decide on your lifetime goals as well as more immediate, short-term goals. Write down all your goals and read them through:

first thing in the morning
sometime during the day
last thing at night.

Remember to repeat the rocking-chair technique at least twice a year to make sure that your goals are still what you really want.

The
POWER
of
HUMOR

"It may seem absurd, at first, to think that it helps to make light of or laugh about your troubles, but you will find that it is in fact one of the best ways of overcoming most stressful situations and creating happiness."

The young man was totally taken aback by this statement. The man before him was Joseph Hart, a small but large-framed man in his late fifties. Mr. Hart was a licensed taxi driver in the city and his was the sixth name on the young man's list.

"Ten years ago," continued Mr. Hart, "my business folded. It didn't take much; I lost my biggest customer, a few large creditors went into liquidation without paying their accounts, and there was just no way out. I saw virtually everything I had worked so hard for being taken from me. Everything was gone.

"As you can imagine, I was angry, frustrated, and

very depressed about the situation. It all seemed so hopeless. I rented a room on the thirtieth floor of the Hilton Hotel in the center of town and, believe it or not, I was going to end my life."

The young man was speechless as he listened to Mr. Hart's story.

"I sat down on the edge of the bed for over half an hour with my head in my hands trying to summon up the courage to do what I had planned. Eventually, I got up and walked out onto the balcony. Just as I reached the edge, I heard a voice behind me. I turned around; a porter had come into the room and asked if everything was all right. I nodded and he came out onto the balcony and asked if he could get me anything. I said no. He looked out at the view of the city. There was a strong breeze and he took a deep breath.

'What a wonderful day!' he said.

'What's so wonderful about it?' I mumbled, and then he said something that hit me like a bucket of iced water.

He said, 'You try missing a few, then you'll find out!'

"I was in such a state of tension that I broke down in tears in front of him. He asked me what was wrong, and I told him that I had lost everything.

He looked puzzled and said, 'What do you mean? Can you still see?'

'Of course,' I said.

'Good, so you still have your eyes. Obviously,' he said, 'you can still talk and hear, and it looks like you can walk, so what exactly have you lost?' I told him it was my money; everything I ever earned had been taken from me. 'Ah!' he exclaimed, 'so all you have lost is your money!' Then he threw another bucket of iced water over me; he said, 'Who has more, a millionaire who has terminal cancer or a healthy man who is penniless?'

"It dawned on me then that perhaps I had blown the problems out of all proportion. The porter explained that many people simply lose perspective of their circumstances and often this is the sole cause of their unhappiness.

"Talking to the porter didn't solve any of my problems, but it did help me to see them a little differently. It was enough to make me think about my life again and, although I never told him, his simple wisdom stopped me from taking my life that day.

"Just before he left, he gave me a list of people who he said would be able to help me with my situation. I thought that they were going to lend me money, but they gave me something much more valuable—the secrets of Abundant Happiness.

"It was through those secrets that I gradually learned to rebuild my life and create happiness for myself. There was a lot I needed to learn about myself and about life—the importance of faith, our attitude, our physical health, forgiveness, relationships—but one of the things that I particularly needed to learn was . . . the power of humor.

"I was one of those people who take everything very seriously. It's not easy being happy if you never laugh!"

"But isn't that putting the cart before the horse?" said the young man. "I mean, we tend to laugh more and take things less seriously when we are happy, not as a means to make us feel happy."

"You are right, laughter *is* a by-product of being happy; but it is also something which *produces* a feeling of happiness. You see, the process of laughing—and smiling for that matter—releases chemicals in your brain which create a kind of euphoria. In fact, researchers have demonstrated that when we laugh, stress hormones in our blood—adrenalin and cortisone—are lowered and, as a result, we actually feel less anxious and less troubled."

"Then why is it that some of the greatest comedians are or were themselves serious depressives?" asked the young man.

"People don't become depressed because they laugh too much," said Mr. Hart. "But many people instinctively use the power of laughter and humor to help them cope with their sadness. Remember that humor is only one of 10 secrets of Abundant Happiness. We need to incorporate all of them into our lives if we are to create lasting happiness. Trying to be happy using only the power of humor is as futile as trying to be healthy by exercising but paying no attention to diet, rest, stress, and all of the other factors that affect our health.

"It has also been shown that laughing improves our powers of concentration and dramatically increases our ability to solve mental problems. Researchers at the University of Maryland conducted a very interesting experiment a few years ago; they took two groups of people and gave them all identical problem-solving tasks. The only difference between the two groups was that the people in one group were first shown a 30-minute educational video before having to do the problem-solving, whereas the people in the other group were shown a 30-minute comedy show. Incredibly, those who watched the comedy solved the problems on average three times faster than the other group!"

The young man looked up from his notes. "But when someone has a problem or is feeling stressed, anxious, or worried," he argued, "they are hardly in the mood to laugh. Are they?"

"No. Of course not. But that's the point! If they did, they could help their situation because not only will they feel better and less stressed, but they will also be more able to resolve their problems. Have you ever experienced something that upset you or made you angry, but a few weeks later you were laughing about it with friends?"

"Yes, hasn't everyone?"

"Did the situation bother you when you were laughing about it?"

"No. How could it?" smiled the young man.

"That is precisely my point," said Mr. Hart. "How could it? It couldn't. So, wouldn't it be easier if we were able to laugh at things sooner rather than later?"

"Yes, I see your point. But how is it possible to laugh about something that is upsetting you?"

"The secret is *finding* something to laugh about. It all goes back to our mind. We choose our thoughts, we choose what we focus our minds on. Instead of focusing on 'What's terrible about this situation?' we can just as easily ask ourselves, 'What's funny about this situation?'"

"What if there is nothing funny?" asked the young man.

"Then ask yourself, 'What *could* be funny?' There is

usually something funny in every situation that you can laugh about, it's just a question of looking for it. And, if there is nothing funny, find something else which is funny because being able to laugh is often half the battle."

"It sounds reasonable in theory, but in practice it's not always easy to find a funny side to every situation," persisted the young man.

"Not every situation can be laughed at," agreed Mr. Hart, "but most can. The thing is—you'll only see the funny side of any situation *if* you look for it. I remember hearing a wonderful story about John Glenn, the first American Apollo astronaut. John was all kitted up ready to enter the rocket when a reporter stopped him. 'John, what's going to happen if, once you're in space, the engines fail and you can't get back down to Earth?' John turned to the reporter and, smiling, said, 'Do you know what? That would really spoil my day!'

"Now I doubt that many people have gone through such a stressful situation as John Glenn faced that day. Probably most of us never will either. But, if we can learn to face life's challenges with the same sense of humor, we would experience more happiness in life.

"After the successful completion of the Apollo mission, a press meeting was held and another reporter asked John what he was thinking about as he was re-entering the Earth's atmosphere. 'What I was thinking about as I was re-entering the atmosphere was that the capsule I was in was manufactured . . . by the lowest bidder!'

"Now that can be a pretty terrifying thought, but John overcame his fears through his humor. It just goes to show that whatever challenges or obstacles confront you in life, one of the best things you can do is ask yourself: 'What is funny about this situation?' or 'What could be funny about it?'

"The problem with most people is that they take life far too seriously. If only we stopped and asked ourselves, 'Will it make any difference to anyone in 10 years' time?' If the answer is 'no', then it doesn't warrant being too serious about, does it? It's a bit like the two-step anti-stress formula."

"What's that?" asked the young man.

"The first step is: don't worry about small things."

There was a pause.

"And the second step?" asked the young man.

"Remember, most things in life are small!

"I have this wonderful piece of prose written by an 85-year-old woman who was terminally ill," said Mr. Hart, handing the young man a piece of paper. "There is great wisdom in it."

If I had my life to live over again, I'd try to make more mistakes next time. I wouldn't be so perfect. I would relax more. I'd limber up. I'd be sillier than I've been on this trip. In fact, I know very few things that I would take so seriously. I'd be crazier. I'd be less hygienic.

I'd take more chances, I'd take more trips, I'd climb more mountains, I'd swim more rivers, I'd go more places I've never been to. I'd eat more ice cream and fewer beans.

I'd have more actual problems but fewer imaginary ones!

You see, I was one of those people who lived

prophylactically and sensibly and sanely hour after hour and day after day. Oh, I've had my moments, and if I had it to do all over again, I'd have more of those moments, moment by moment.

I've been one of those people who never went anywhere without a thermometer, a hot water bottle, a gargle, a raincoat and a parachute. If I had to do it all over again, I'd travel lighter next time.

If I had to do it all over again, I'd start barefoot earlier in the spring and stay that way later in the fall. I'd ride more merry-go-rounds, I'd watch more sunrises, and I'd play with more children, if I had my life to live over again.

But you see, I don't.

The young man smiled as he read it. "You're right. There's a wonderful message there. Can I have a copy?"

"Of course," said Mr. Hart.

"Thank you for sharing all this with me," said the young man. "You've given me a lot to think about."

"Good. I'm pleased I have been able to help," said Mr. Hart. "Before you go, did I tell you what George Burns said was the secret of happiness?"

"No."

"'The secret of happiness?' he said. 'Simple. A good cigar, a good meal, and a good woman—or a bad woman. It depends upon how much happiness you can handle!'"

As the young man reached the door, he turned back to Mr. Hart. "You didn't mention how you knew the old Chinese man who gave me your name?"

Mr. Hart smiled. "Didn't I tell you? He was the porter at the hotel. I never told him what I had been planning to do that day. The following morning I went to the hotel reception to thank him and let him know how much he had helped me, but nobody had heard of him."

"So you never got to thank him then?" asked the young man.

"No. No, I didn't," said Mr. Hart with a smile. "But I have a feeling that he knows. After all, he gave you my name, didn't he?"

That night, before going to bed, the young man read over his notes.

The sixth secret of Abundant Happiness—the power of humor.

Humor alleviates stress and creates feelings of happiness.

Laughing improves our powers of concentration and increases our ability to solve problems.

In any experience, if you look for a funny side, very often you'll find one.

Instead of asking, "What's terrible about this situation?" ask, "What's funny about it?" or "What could be funny?"

Always refer to the two-step anti-stress formula:

Don't worry about small things
Remember most things are small!

The
POWER
of
FORGIVENESS

The next day the young man sat in the office of the seventh person on his list, a man by the name of Dr. Howard Jacobson. Dr. Jacobson was a tall, large-framed man with fair hair and bright blue eyes and, at 42 years old, he was the youngest Chief Surgeon ever to be appointed at the city hospital. His office was on the top floor of the building and the two exterior walls were entirely made of glass, giving a magnificent panoramic view to the west of the city.

"I first heard about the secrets of Abundant Happiness 20 years ago," said Dr. Jacobson.

"And did they help you?" asked the young man.

"Most definitely," said Dr. Jacobson. "They completely changed my outlook on life. I was never very happy growing up," confided Dr. Jacobson. "I was always 'going-to-be' happy. Originally, I was going to be happy when I got to college, but when I got there nothing changed. Then I thought that I'd be happy when I qualified as a doctor, but that didn't work either. Neither did anything change when I qualified as a surgeon, or when I got married and had children. But, the truth is, despite being successful and having a nice home with a loving wife and family, I was never really happy.

"Looking back, I think my problems all began when I was sent off at the age of 10 to boarding school by my father—against my wishes. My mother had died in a car crash a year earlier. She died on impact, so I was told, but my father, who had been driving, survived with hardly a scratch. I think that subconsciously I blamed him for the accident and, although it's a terrible thing to admit, I grew to hate him."

"Why?" asked the young man.

"I suppose I thought that he had sent me away to boarding school because he didn't love me or want me at home."

Dr. Jacobson paused for a moment and looked out of the window.

"I lived with this anger for over 15 years," he said, and then, his voice lowered, "It's difficult being happy when you're carrying so much anger and resentment inside.

"Then one day I was at the airport on my way to a conference when a message came over the loudspeakers—'Would Dr. Jacobson please report to the information desk?' I went along, and was handed an urgent message—my father had had a heart attack and was in the intensive care unit of the city hospital. I sat down and re-read the message, confused, unsure what to do. I hadn't even spoken to him for over five years.

"I screwed up the piece of paper in my hand and was about to throw it in the bin next to me when someone asked if the seat beside me was free. I looked up and there he was ... a little old Chinese man. He sat down and immediately started talking. He was on his way to visit a friend who had lost a leg in an accident. A car had hit him whilst he was crossing the road at traffic lights and completely smashed the man's right leg. He was lucky to be alive. It transpired that the driver of the car had been in a hurry and hadn't seen the man begin to cross the road. 'I hate people like that,' I said, but the man next to me looked horrified. 'Why hate a man just because he made a mistake?' he asked. 'Everyone makes mistakes at one time or another in their lives. If you hate every person who makes a mistake, you'll end up hating everybody ... including yourself.'

"Then he turned toward me and, smiling, looked me squarely in the eye and said, 'We have a saying in my country, "Those who will not forgive, will not be happy."'

"'It's not always easy to forgive,' I argued. 'It depends upon how bad the mistake is.'

"'If that is so,' he said, 'heaven would be a very lonely place.'

"He talked for a few more minutes and mentioned the laws of life and the secrets of Abundant Happiness. I had never heard such things before but hearing them stirred something inside me. A few minutes later, the old man had left me as he found me—staring at the screwed up message in my hand. But now I knew what I wanted to do.

"I canceled my trip and went instead to visit my father in hospital. He was lying in bed with tubes all around him and a heart monitor beside his bed. I went over to his side, sat down on the edge of the bed and did something I hadn't done since I was a child . . . I held his hand. He lay there motionless, not even able to speak, and the doctors weren't sure whether he could hear either. I bent over him and whispered in his ear, 'Dad, it's me. It's Howard.' Then the most beautiful thing I have ever experienced happened. A tear began to roll down his cheek and, for the first time in many, many years, I wept. It was time to forgive and let go of the past.

"Over the next two weeks I visited him every day, and although his eyes remained closed, when I held his hand his eyelids flickered very slightly and he gripped my hand tightly. Then, at last, the miracle that I had been praying for happened. I arrived at the hospital and found him fully awake and drinking a cup of tea.

"We hugged—something we hadn't done since I was a young child—and we talked. We talked more in that one afternoon than we had done in the previous 15 years. And it was only then that I learned about the accident that killed my mother and why I had been sent to boarding school against my wishes. A lorry had skidded out of control on black ice and smashed into the passenger door, killing my mother on impact. It was nobody's fault; it was an accident. And although he never showed it at the time, my father had been devastated. It still brought tears to his eyes to talk about it. My mother and he were child-hood sweethearts. I had never stopped even once to think of the pain he had been going through, I had only thought of myself. He had a highly paid job, but it involved him in frequently traveling to the Far East and America and, right or wrong, he thought I would be better off and receive a better education if I was at a boarding school.

"People say that time heals, but it doesn't. It's true that anger and bitterness usually fade over the years, but unless we are prepared to forgive, they never totally leave your soul. No, the key to forgiveness doesn't lie in the passing of time, it lies in under-standing. The Sioux Indians have a wonderful prayer:

O Great Spirit, keep me from ever judging and criticizing a man until I have walked in his mocassins for two weeks.

"We often blame people for things, but we can never be sure that, given the same upbringing and circumstances, we would react any differently to another person. For instance, I had never thought of what my father might be going through after the death of my mother or why he had insisted I go to boarding school. I had only chosen to see it from my point of view. Subconsciously, I thought that by placing me in a boarding school, my father didn't want me or love me. But it turned out he did it *because* he loved me. He thought it was for the best. He had also lost my mother—his childhood sweet-heart—and he didn't know how to take care of me and wasn't able to take care of me because of his work commitments."

The young man thought about his own life. There were plenty of people who angered him. His boss, who was always harassing him, and a close friend who borrowed money over a year ago and still hadn't repaid it, were two that immediately came to mind. It suddenly occurred to him that he hadn't even considered the matters from their point of view.

"I can see that when no malice is involved, things should be forgiven, but if someone intentionally harms you, why should you forgive them?" asked the young man.

"Why not?"

"Because some things are just unforgivable!" argued the young man.

"I'm not so sure," said Dr. Jacobson. "Take child molesters as an example. You can't get a more heinous and repugnant crime, can you?"

The young man nodded.

"Yet, did you know that over 95 percent of all child molesters were themselves molested when they were children? Can you be certain, if you had suffered in the same way, that you wouldn't have committed the same crimes?"

The young man shook his head. "I suppose not, but it's not so easy forgiving."

"No one said it was easy. You know what they say? 'To err is human, but to forgive is divine!' But it helps if we try looking at things from the other person's view. And look what happens if you can't forgive? Who suffers? Who gets the stomach ulcers and the high blood pressure? You do!"

"Not if you get even first. Even the Bible says, 'An eye for an eye and a tooth for a tooth.' Isn't revenge good for the soul?"

"The Bible also says, 'Turn the other cheek' and 'Leave revenge to God.' If we sought revenge every time we were wronged, as Mahatma Gandhi once said, 'The whole world would end up being blind and toothless.' Revenge cannot bring peace, it only breeds more revenge. It's a never-ending cycle.

"If your heart is full of hatred, how can there be room for love and happiness? Forgiveness frees your soul from hatred and allows room for love to enter."

Dr. Jacobson walked over to the far side of the room where there were two high-backed chairs against the wall.

"It's like these chairs," he said. "One is love and happiness, the other resentment and anger. You can't carry both at the same time."

"Well, you can forgive, but not forget," insisted the young man.

"That is not forgiveness. Forgiveness is wiping the slate clean, completely erasing it. It's letting go of the anger and condemnation, just like letting go of a heavy rock. Carrying the rock will weigh you down; let it go and it has no power over you, you are free. This is why Confucius said, 'To be wronged or robbed is nothing, unless you continue to remember it.'

"Every religion in the world speaks of the power of forgiveness. How can we expect God to forgive us if we cannot forgive others? A man who cannot forgive burns the bridge over which he will have to pass himself, because we all at some time need to be forgiven."

"But how many times can you forgive someone?"

"As many times as he wrongs you. Always remember, the only person who suffers if you don't forgive is you, because it will be you who carries the hatred and anger and resentment. Forgiveness frees you from that suffering. This is why it is so vital if you want to be happy. It is only by letting go of condemning judgments and grievances that we are free to experience joy and happiness. I believe that, in time, every man must pay the penalty for his own misdeeds, either in this life or the next. If there is one law in this universe it is the law of cause and effect or, as it is written: 'We reap what we sow'—our actions come back to us. If you believe this you no longer need to hold on to anger or bitterness or hatred. Of course, I don't know for certain if the universe works this way—I may be wrong—but I choose to believe it and I'm happier for it.

"But, do you know who is the hardest person to forgive, the one person who you will find it most difficult to be compassionate to?" continued Dr. Jacobson.

"No."

"Yourself!"

"What do you mean. Why should I need to forgive myself?"

"Whenever you make a mistake or do something you later regret. We need to remember that everyone is doing the best they can most of the time. We are humans and humans slip up and make mistakes. We all do things at times that we are ashamed of or embarrassed by and wish we could change.

"Every now and again it helps to step aside and see yourself the way you once were as a little child. Be gentle with that child. How can you be happy if you don't love and respect yourself. If God can forgive you, you can forgive yourself. There is an old proverb—'The wise man falls down seven times each day, but he also stands up seven times.'"

"I had never thought of it this way before," said the young man. "It sounds all well and good, but I don't think it is necessarily an easy path to follow. All I can do is try."

Before he went to bed that night, the young man read over his notes.

The seventh secret of Abundant Happiness—the power of forgiveness.

Forgiveness is the key which opens the door to Abundant Happiness.

You can't be happy if you carry feelings of hatred or resentment. Remember no one suffers from your bitterness but you.

Mistakes and failures are life's lessons. Forgive yourself and forgive others.

Remember the Sioux Indian prayer:

"O Great Spirit, keep me from ever judging and criticizing a man until I have walked in his mocassins for two weeks."

The
POWER
of
GIVING

Two days later the young man sat in the spectators'
gallery overlooking the swimming pool at the community sports center, waiting to meet the next person
on his list, a man by the name of Peter Tansworth.
The gallery was empty but the young man could hear
the screams and shouts of children splashing about in
the pool.

"Hello. Are you the man I spoke to on the telephone last week?" shouted a man wearing a tracksuit
by the poolside.

"Mr. Tansworth?"

"That's me," said the man in the tracksuit smiling
up at the young man.

"I'll be with you shortly. Ten minutes or so. We're
just finishing off."

"No problem!" shouted the young man. "You
carry on."

The scene seemed very ordinary to the young man. Nothing unusual about 20 or so children enjoying a swimming lesson. But as the children began to get out of the pool, the young man noticed one little boy had only one arm, then another had no legs. As he looked around, he observed that all of the children were physically handicapped.

A few minutes later Mr. Tansworth joined the young man in the gallery.

"Hi. Pleased to meet you at last," Mr. Tansworth said, shaking the young man's hand.

Mr. Tansworth had a slightly tanned complexion and large smiling eyes. The young man told him of his meeting with the old Chinese man and of the people he had subsequently met.

"When I met the old man—almost five years ago now—it also turned out to be a major turning point in my life," said Mr. Tansworth. "At that time, I owned a successful computer company. I was doing very well in the business. Making money had always been my main aim in life and when I reached my 35th birthday, I was a millionaire . . . but I was also very unhappy."

"Why?" asked the young man.

"You know it is written: 'What shall it profit a man if he shall gain the whole world, but lose his soul?' That just about sums up what my life was like. In my rise to the top I had left behind the things which really mattered to me: my wife divorced me, I had only a few friends, and every day was simply a battle to acquire more money than I could ever spend.

"I remember one Christmas I was feeling so miserable that I bought myself a Rolex watch to cheer myself up. It cost over $7,500 and for a while I was very proud of my new acquisition. But within half an hour the feeling had worn off and I felt just as miserable as I had been without it. Looking back I can't imagine why I thought a watch would make me happy; it was the same as most other watches—all it did was tell me the time.

"I remember that day well. It was Christmas Eve . . . the streets were bursting with people and I sat down on a bench in a shopping mall, watching the frantic bustle of people. Although I was sitting among thousands of people who were passing me by, I have never felt so totally alone. I became overwhelmed with a terrible feeling of loneliness.

"Christmas can be a wonderful time of year, but it can also be a very miserable and lonely time. Every year hundreds of thousands of people sit in misery—those with no family or friends; those with no money, no food, and those who are homeless. For them, Christmas is a time that only magnifies their lack. That day I got my first glimpse of how miserable and lonely life can be, but then something happened that changed the rest of my life."

"What was that?" asked the young man.

"A little old Chinese man sat down beside me!"

The young man smiled.

"He turned to me and said, 'Did you know that the only time during the four years of fighting in the First World War when soldiers put down their guns and made peace was Christmas 1914?' I had no idea nor much interest, but he continued regardless. 'British and German soldiers climbed out of their trenches and greeted one another in No Man's Land and shared food and drink.'"

Mr. Tansworth paused and then added, "It's incredible when you think about it, isn't it?"

The young man nodded, "Yes. I suppose it is."

"The old man then said, 'All the year round people pursue happiness in having and acquiring, and getting served by others, but it takes a time like Christmas to remind us that real happiness is found in giving and in serving.'

"The old man's words really made me think about my life. I had always thought that it was by acquiring things that we became happy—acquiring more money, a better job, a bigger house, and a faster car. But the fact remained that even though I had acquired everything I had set out to possess, I was still unhappy.

"I had a long discussion with the old man and that was the first time I had ever heard of the 10 secrets of Abundant Happiness. Through him I met some wonderful people who shared those secrets with me and all of them helped enrich my life. But there was one secret that was particularly important to me, and that was . . . the power of giving.

"It is incredible to think that the one thing we crave most in life—happiness—we can get most easily—by giving it away. It is one of the most magical laws in Nature—the more you give, the more you receive. It's like sowing seeds, for every seed you sow, you'll get thousands back."

"But how can you give away something you haven't got?" asked the young man.

Mr. Tansworth smiled. "That's the beauty of it!" he exclaimed. "You can get it *by* giving it away. When you give joy, you instantly receive it. It's like perfume."

"Perfume?" repeated the young man.

"You can't pour it on others without getting a few drops on yourself. Take smiling: if you smile at someone, invariably they will smile back. You see, happiness is like a boomerang—the more you give it away, the more it comes back to you.

"I am sure you can remember a time when you did something for someone else with no ulterior motive, even a small thing like giving someone who is lost directions or helping a blind person cross the street, or simply remembering a friend's birthday? Or giving someone a sincere compliment or showing your appreciation and thanking them?"

The young man nodded, "Yes. Of course."

"Didn't that make you feel good inside? Not just because the person might have been grateful for what you said or did, but simply because it feels good to do something for or to help a fellow human being."

The young man thought about the time a few years back when he had been approached by a foreign woman who was lost in the city and needed directions. The address she was seeking was three kilometers away; it was the middle of winter and snowing, and the woman was shivering. There was no way she would have been able to find her way there, not in such terrible weather. So he drove her to where she wanted to go. And now, looking back, he remembered how good he had felt about himself at the time.

"You see, deep down human beings are not by their nature selfish. We will do far more for other people than we will do for ourselves. Most parents, for instance, will willingly sacrifice their own comfort for the sake of their children.

"After talking to the old Chinese man in the shopping mall that day, I walked along the mall and came across a Salvation Army choir singing Christmas carols. There was a big sign saying, 'Help the homeless this Christmas.' Almost without thinking about it, I took the Rolex watch back to the shop and instead gave a check for $7,500 to a Salvation Army collector. And do you know I will never forget the look of astonishment and gratitude on the woman's face. She showed it to her colleague and tears came to her eyes. 'This will make such a difference,' she said. 'Thank you and may God bless you.' And it was then that I first began to understand what the old man had said because I got more pleasure from giving away that check and knowing that I had made a difference, however small, in other people's lives than I would have got from wearing the watch for a lifetime.

"I remember reading some years back how a father wanted to teach his son the value of giving from an early age. It was his son's sixth birthday and he had been given lots of brightly colored helium balloons by his grandmother. After the party, the father told his son that he had an idea how he could have even more fun with the balloons . . . by giving some of them away! Needless to say, the boy wasn't too enthusiastic about this suggestion but the father assured him that he would have fun and, reluctantly, the boy agreed.

"They went to an old folks' home and the little boy walked into the lounge carrying 20 helium balloons and gave one to every person in the room. Suddenly people were laughing and talking excitedly, and one old lady who hadn't had a visitor for over three years was so moved that she wept. It was as if the little boy had turned on a light switch and lit up the room. They all told him how wonderful he was to think of them, and soon everyone in the room was laughing and wanting a hug from him. And that little boy loved every minute of it, so much so that on the way home he asked his father when they could go back and do it again. It was a lesson the little boy never forgot; from that day on, he always looked for opportunities to give rather than only to take."

"That's a wonderful story," said the young man.

"Let me tell you another one which particularly moved me," said Mr. Tansworth. "A few years ago I met a man named Paul who told me how he had learned the power of giving when he was still a college student. Paul had been given a brand new car for his eighteenth birthday by his older brother and naturally he drove it to college to show it off. One of the juniors walked around the shiny new car admiring it. 'What do you think?' Paul said. 'It's fantastic!' enthused the junior. 'Fantastic!' And when Paul told him that it was a birthday present from his older brother, the junior was dumbfounded. 'Your brother gave it to you?' he said. 'Wow. I wish . . . ' Paul knew what the junior was going to say: 'I wish I had a brother like that.' But what the junior actually said was something quite different and his words stayed with Paul for the rest of his life. The boy said: 'I wish I could *be* a brother like that!'

"Paul was so taken with what the little boy had said that he offered to give him a ride in the car during the lunch break. The junior couldn't hide his excitement and asked if they could stop by his house. Paul smiled to himself. He thought he knew what the boy wanted; he wanted to show his friends and neighbors that he had driven in a brand new car.

"Ten minutes later the car stopped outside the junior's house and the little boy ran inside. The next moment he came back out pushing a little boy in a wheelchair. 'Wow!' said the little boy with wide open eyes. And then something happened that brought tears to Paul's eyes. The junior said to his little brother: 'Some day, Sam, I'm gonna buy you a car just like that one.' Hearing this, Paul said, 'Say, Sam, would you like to come for a ride as well?' And he lifted the tiny crippled boy into the car and then the three of them went for a drive. And, that day, the proud owner of the new car was humbled and understood for the first time in his life why it is written: 'It is more blessed to give than to receive.'

"So you see," said Mr. Tansworth, "by giving of ourselves to others, we don't merely take our minds off our own problems. To me it is the greatest secret of Abundant Happiness: all you have to do to bring happiness and joy into your life is to give it to others.

"This is why I always look for places and people to whom I could give help; not just money, but my time as well. That's how I ended up with this job, teaching handicapped children how to swim. It makes me happy to be able to make a difference in their lives. I don't believe there's any greater happiness than that which we get when we are able to help or bring joy to another human being."

On his way home the young man thought about what Mr. Tansworth had said in relation to his own life. The past few years he had been too wrapped up in his own problems to worry about other people's. The thought had never occurred to him that by considering other people and taking the time to do something for them, particularly those closest to him, he would in fact be helping himself.

When he arrived home that evening the young man summarized his notes.

The eighth secret of Abundant Happiness—the power of giving.

Happiness is not found in having and acquiring for ourselves, but in giving to and helping others.

The more joy and happiness we give, the more we receive.

Every day I can create happiness in my own life by looking for ways to bring happiness to others.

The
POWER
of
RELATIONSHIPS

Two days later the young man met the next person on his list in a small coffee shop in the center of town. Ed Hansen lived alone in a small apartment on the east side of the city. He had not always lived alone; at one time he had lived in a four-bedroomed detached house with his wife and two children, but that was a long time ago, before the drinking started.

"I can't complain," Mr. Hansen said to the young man. "I messed up, I have nobody else to blame but myself. In fact, I'm grateful for having a second chance. I've been sober now for 10 years."

"How did it all begin?" asked the young man.

"It started many, many years ago. The stress and pressure of work, worries, anxiety; you know what it's like. One evening I stopped in a local bar to have a drink with a few colleagues after work. All I had was a few glasses of wine, just to relax and unwind a little. It worked as well and the following evening I stopped off again. Before I knew it, I was drinking a bottle of wine every evening after work and soon that increased to two or three. It didn't take very long—a few months maybe—before I was drinking during the day as well. As you can imagine, my life fell to pieces; my work deteriorated rapidly and I was given the sack, my wife took the children and left me, I couldn't pay the bills and a few months later I was evicted. The rest is a bit of a blur. I ended up homeless and living on the streets, begging."

The young man was shocked by Mr. Hansen's story. He had never met someone who had been homeless before; he had always assumed that homeless people were outcasts and misfits, different from everyone else, but Mr. Hansen seemed so normal. It humbled him to realize that anyone who was desperately unhappy or couldn't cope with their worries or daily stresses could so easily find themselves in the same predicament. "There but for the grace of God go I," he thought as he took a sip from his coffee.

"How did you manage to turn your life around?" he asked.

"It wasn't easy. I did it with help. At the time I would never have admitted that I needed help, but I did. I felt trapped, completely powerless. I remember one winter's night I was so cold, so freezing, that not even the booze could numb the pain. I really thought that I was going to die. I hadn't eaten for three days and I lay huddled and shivering in a cardboard box. All I could do was pray that my end would come quickly and painlessly.

"The next thing I remember, someone was standing

over me. It was too dark to see who it was, but he had a soft, gentle voice. He said, 'Come with me, Ed, it's time for you to leave here,' and he held out his hand. I thought that perhaps I had died because as soon as he touched me, all of the pain in my body vanished. He led me down the street and after a few minutes we stopped in front of a large building. I turned to face him; he was an old Chinese man. He handed me a piece of paper and said, 'This is it, Ed. This is where your new life begins. Be well.' I looked at the paper he had given me, but when I looked up again, he was gone."

The young man had already guessed who Ed's mysterious rescuer had been, but still felt a lump rise in his throat and his eyes begin to glaze.

"There was a meeting going on in the building," continued Mr. Hansen. "An Alcoholics Anonymous meeting. But it was warm and there was a wonderful smell of hot coffee, so I stayed. I looked at the piece of paper the old man had given to me and . . . "

"There was a list of 10 names?" interjected the young man.

"Yes," answered Mr. Hansen, smiling, "but the amazing thing was . . . the last name on my list was the same name on the blackboard. It was the name of the speaker, Mr. John Mapland.

"After the meeting I went over to Mr. Mapland and showed him the piece of paper. He then put his arm around me and said, 'Don't worry, Ed, we're all friends here. If you need help, this is where you'll get it.' That evening I began to live again just as the old man had promised. Despite my bedraggled appearance, everyone was very friendly. For the first time, people were willing to listen to me without being critical or judgmental.

"I regularly attended the AA meetings and, with time and determination and the grace of God, I regained my sobriety. During that time I met the other people on the list the old man had given me and they inspired me and showed me how to live again with the secrets of Abundant Happiness. All of the secrets helped me in some way, and enriched my life. But the one that saved my life that night was . . . the power of relationships."

"Relationships? What do you mean?" said the young man.

"Unconditional, loving relationships. Without relationships, life is empty. After all, life is meant to be a celebration and it's not much fun having a party by yourself, is it?

"Human beings are social creatures. We need to talk, we need to communicate, we need to feel wanted and needed. We all need each other. It is even written in the Bible: 'It is not good for man to be alone.'

"When I look back," explained Mr. Hansen, "I can see now how I neglected my friends and family in my struggle to succeed in business. Perhaps that was one of the reasons I began drinking in the first place. I don't know much, but I do know that I would never have been able to overcome my problems without the love and support of a room full of strangers, all of whom understood what I had been through and all of whom accepted me for what I was and offered me help without asking for anything in return. Sometimes in life you can find yourself in a hole so deep that you simply can't climb out alone.

It's at times like those that you need someone to pull you up."

Mr. Hansen paused momentarily.

"If you were to ask me what lessons I have learned in life, right up at the top of the list would be this: the quality of our lives is the quality of our relationships."

"In what way?" asked the young man.

"Well, happiness arises first from your relationship with yourself, but then from the friendship and love of your relationships with other people. After all, how much pleasure would there be if you could only do things alone?"

"It's very true," said the young man. "Last year I went on holiday by myself to the Seychelles and although everything was wonderful, there was definitely something missing. It wasn't the same as having someone there with you to share it with."

"Exactly," said Mr. Hansen, "having other people you care about makes good experiences even better, but they also make the difficult times easier. Have you ever noticed how you automatically feel better after you have talked to somebody about your problems? They may not have given you any advice or tangible help, and you still may have the problem, but somehow, it doesn't feel quite so bad?"

The young man nodded. There were plenty of times when he had talked over problems with a friend and felt better for it.

"But something that you may not have noticed," continued Mr. Hansen, "is that we tend to become most anxious or worried or depressed or unhappy when we keep our thoughts to ourselves. If we keep our problems to ourselves we can easily blow them out of proportion and gradually they seem to get worse and we start to feel overwhelmed and powerless. The old saying 'Two heads are better than one' is absolutely true, not just because there is double the brain power to help find a solution to a problem, but also because the process of sharing problems, worries, or anxieties often relieves them.

"Relationships enrich our lives. If you share joy, you multiply joy, but if you share a problem, you halve a problem. Lord Byron, the English poet, put it this way:

All who joy would win,
Must share it—Happiness was born a twin."

It all made sense to the young man. He had always kept his problems to himself. Although he had close friends and family, he rarely discussed his problems with them. But the truth was, he had never found it easy developing close relationships.

"It's all very well," he said, "and I understand what you mean, but some people find relationships difficult."

"If you find relationships difficult, you will invariably find life difficult," said Mr. Hansen.

"Yes," agreed the young man, "but for instance, in my case, I have always been a bit of a loner. I've never found it easy making friends or developing close relationships."

"Have you ever heard the phrase: 'The past is not the future'?"

"No."

"What it means is that just because something

happened yesterday, doesn't mean it has to happen again tomorrow. Just because you had problems with relationships in the past doesn't mean that you have to have the same problems in the future. It might mean that in the past you were simply going about it in the wrong way."

"What do you mean?" asked the young man.

"Well, what makes you like someone?"

"I don't know. Sometimes I click with another person and sometimes I don't."

"Okay. Let's look at it another way; do you feel at ease with someone who looks you in the eye when you meet them or someone who avoids eye contact?"

"Someone who looks me in the eye."

"Good. And are you more comfortable with someone who has a firm handshake or someone whose grip feels like a wet squid?"

"Firm handshake."

"Of course. And do you prefer a person to only talk about themselves or to be interested in you as well?"

"I'd prefer someone who was interested in me," said the young man. "But this is all obvious."

"You're right," said Mr. Hansen, "it is obvious, but do you consciously do these things when you first meet people? You'd be surprised how many people don't, and then wonder why they have difficulty developing relationships with other people."

The young man looked away briefly. "You're right. If I'm honest, I don't think I've ever really thought about it."

"And, if we want to keep our friends, we need to learn to accept them for who they are and overlook what we may see as their shortcomings, and instead focus on their positive or admirable qualities. We have to be willing to forgive them when they make mistakes, just as we would want them to forgive us ours."

"Yes," said the young man, "I had a long chat with a man about the power of forgiveness last week."

"Forgiveness is very important in being happy," said Mr. Hansen, "because without it we would end up alone and bitter. When we value our relationships, we automatically treat people differently. And, when we treat people well, they tend to treat us well."

"But still, relationships are not always easy, are they?" said the young man. "There are bound to be problems and disagreements in any relationship."

"Of course there are. But I found one simple technique that helps all my relationships."

"What's that?" asked the young man.

"I always try to treat everyone I meet as if I might never see them again. Can you imagine how your relationships with your friends, your work colleagues, your family, and even strangers might change if you treated everyone you met as if it was the last time you would see them?"

The young man shook his head. "I'm not with you."

"How would you behave to your wife or girlfriend if you thought you might not see her again? Would you let her leave you without kissing or hugging her?"

"No."

"Would you say 'goodbye' with an unresolved argument?"

"No."

"Would you let them go without telling them how much they meant to you?"

"No."

"And what about work colleagues or friends or members of your family? If you thought you might never see someone again, wouldn't you try to make your time with them as memorable as possible? Wouldn't you do your utmost to avoid parting with bad feeling?"

The young man nodded. Mr. Hansen's words struck a chord deep within him. It brought back his memory of the last time he saw his mother. It was a hot summer's day and she was leaving for a holiday abroad. He was in a hurry to meet his friends for a game of tennis, and quickly gave his mother a peck on the cheek. He had no way of knowing that she would never return and that was to be their final farewell. He had thought about it often since; it was the moment in his life that he most regretted, and would for the rest of his life. He understood now how to avoid making the same mistake with other people who he cared about and loved. It was simple, as Mr. Hansen had said, "Treat people as if you may never see them again."

"Many people," said Mr. Hansen, "simply don't value their relationships. I chose my career over my family and in doing so, lost both. Others choose money and possessions over their relationships. You'd be surprised how many brothers, sisters, parents, and children are willing to fall out over money. They sacrifice their closest relationships and unknowingly sacrifice their happiness as well."

Later that evening, the young man summarized the notes he had made that day.

The ninth secret of Abundant Happiness—the power of relationships.

The quality of my life is the quality of my relationships.

No man is an island. We all need relationships.

Close relationships make the good times better and the difficult times easier. A joy shared is a joy doubled, but a problem shared is a problem halved.

Treat everyone you meet as if you may never see them again.

The
POWER
of
FAITH

It was another week before the young man was able to meet with the last person on his list. During that time he had the opportunity of reviewing and practicing some of the things he had learned. He made happiness a priority and always tried to look for positive things in every difficult situation. He had also begun using the power of his body, particularly exercising regularly and taking care of his diet.

He had found the secret of living in the moment especially beneficial at work. He had noticed that he was getting more done, more successfully, with less stress or worry. Even his boss noticed the change in the young man's performance and praised him for his efforts. The young man repeated positive affirmations to himself every day to help improve his self-image and, by asking himself five empowering questions at the start of each day, he found he was more enthusiastic, more eager to face the challenges of each day.

He had used the rocking-chair technique, setting lifetime goals as well as shorter-term goals and he wrote each one of them down and read them all three times each day to keep them imprinted on his mind. He found that he had much more energy and enthusiasm when he had things to strive for and look forward to.

The young man had also begun to take himself less seriously and consciously looked for the funny side of events, especially in stressful situations. At the same time, he made sure that he treated everyone he met as if he might never see them again, and consequently he found himself treating people more considerately and he noticed that they in return treated him the same way. He never let an opportunity pass without letting the people around him—his friends, his family, his work colleagues—know that he appreciated them.

One major difference that the young man noticed immediately was that by looking for ways he could help and give to others he spread happiness and received it at the same time. He found that bringing a smile to someone else always made him feel good as well. It was a wonderful feeling making a difference to someone else's life.

And at the end of each day, the young man made it a rule to try and forgive anybody who had upset him that day. This way he found he never went to sleep with any feelings of bitterness or resentment.

Yes, there was no doubt that he was feeling more energetic, more enthusiastic, and happier than he had ever been. There was no doubt in his mind that the secrets of Abundant Happiness were really working!

"What then," he thought to himself, "could the last person on my list possibly add to what I have already learned?"

Miss June Henderson lived in a small apartment in the suburbs a few kilometers north of the city. She was a pretty woman, still in her early forties, very petite, with auburn shoulder-length hair and large green eyes.

"So, you met the old man," Miss Henderson said to the young man.

"Yes. He turned up a few weeks ago when my car broke down."

"It is amazing, isn't it, that at times when you least expect it, something wonderful happens?" said Miss Henderson.

"I suppose so," said the young man.

"It is called the eleventh-hour principle. Have you heard of it?"

"No," said the young man, shaking his head.

"Well, it is simply that just as the night is often darkest and coldest just before the dawn, it is when things look really bleak that we often experience a dramatic turn for the better and something wonderful happens.

"The old Chinese man always turns up at the eleventh hour."

"I suppose that's true," replied the young man.

"When I met the old man I was very unhappy," said Miss Henderson.

"Why?" asked the young man.

"My mother had died only a month before. I can still remember it as if it were yesterday."

The young man was embarrassed for asking the question. "I'm sorry," he said.

"Thank you, it's okay. Really. I was only 21 at the time and I had just finished my final year's exams at university. It was a terrible shock. My mother, despite being a heavy smoker, had always enjoyed good health, but these things eventually take their toll. She died suddenly—had a heart attack—whilst on holiday.

"One day I was sitting alone on the veranda outside our apartment thinking about her. I don't know how long I had been there before I became aware that I was not alone. On the balcony of the neighboring apartment was an elderly Chinese man. Our eyes met, he smiled and said, 'Hello,' and we began talking. It was very strange; I had never met him before but it felt as if I had known him for years."

The young man recalled how he had also felt comfortable talking about intimate details of his life with the old man within five minutes of meeting him.

"The old man was so wise and gentle," said Miss Henderson. "He seemed to know that something was wrong and funnily enough it was him who brought the conversation around to the subject of death. He explained that in his country, death is a time of celebration, not one of sorrow."

"How can losing someone you love and will never see again be a time to celebrate?" asked the bewildered young man.

"I asked exactly the same question," said Miss Henderson. "And the old man explained the golden rule of happiness."

"Oh, yes. He told me as well," said the young man. "Our attitudes and beliefs determine our feelings, not our circumstances."

"Exactly," said Miss Henderson smiling. "The old man explained that, in his country, they believe that our existence began a long time before we were born into this world. Our short life in this world is merely a school of learning from which we graduate when we are ready. So, when a person dies, their soul continues on its journey. All of the major religions share the belief that while the body may die, the spirit lives on and in another time and another place, we will meet our loved ones again. Even the Bible describes death as 'sleep' from which, one day, we will all awake."

Miss Henderson pointed to a plaque on the wall next to the young man.

"I first read these words in a cemetery on a 300-year-old headstone," she said. The plaque read:

There is an old belief,
That on some solemn shore,
Beyond the sphere of grief,
Dear friends shall meet once more.

"If you believe death to be a final and complete separation, then it can be devastating. But if you believe that the separation is only temporary, and that the soul lives on, it is not quite so distressing."

"But, even though death may not be permanent, any separation is sad, isn't it?" said the young man.

"Yes, even a temporary separation can be sad," said Miss Henderson, "although in some eastern faiths they are joyful because they believe the soul of the person has returned to its true home, on to a higher level of learning.

"But, talking to the old man that day did more than

just help me come to terms with my grief, it made me review all of my beliefs."

"In what way?" asked the young man.

"Well, you might not believe it but I used to be a terrible worrier," she said. "When I was only 12 years old I worried about the fact that one day I was going to die! Can you believe it? I worried about everything; things I had said or done, the things I had to do, things that had gone wrong and things that might go wrong. And if I had nothing to worry about I worried that there was something I should be worried about!"

The young man could empathize with this. He spent most of his days worrying about one thing or another—deadlines at work, bills, his health—there was always something that might go wrong.

"Sitting there, talking to the old man," continued Miss Henderson, "made me realize the insignificance of most of the things I had always worried about. Faced with the death of the one person closest to me, all worries about bills, mortgages, exams, jobs . . . everything fades into insignificance.

"The old man introduced me to the secrets of Abundant Happiness and I can honestly say that those secrets changed my life. It was a revelation for me. I had never considered that I was the architect of my own happiness or misery. I learned, for instance, the importance of my attitude and beliefs, the effect of my body on my emotions, the power of a strong self-image, the necessity of goals and a sense of humor, and I learned to value each day and try to live in the moment. But, the one secret that I think I most needed to learn and which therefore had the most profound effect on my life was . . . the power of faith."

"Faith?" repeated the young man. "What does faith have to do with happiness?"

"We all need a certain amount of faith just to live, let alone be happy," replied Miss Henderson. "Let me give you an example. Do you drive a car?"

"Yes."

"How do you know that your car is safe to drive?"

"I had it serviced only a month ago."

"How do you know the mechanic did his job properly?"

"Erm . . . I don't know for sure, but . . . "

"So you must have faith in the mechanic.

"And when you drive, how can you be sure that you won't have an accident?"

"I drive carefully," said the young man.

"So, you have faith in your own ability to drive. That's good, but there might be other drivers on the road who are not careful, mightn't there?"

"Possibly," admitted the young man, "but I think most people are careful."

"So, you also have faith in other road users. Can you see that, in order to drive your car, you have to have faith in the people who manufactured and serviced the car, other drivers on the road, and yourself. You can imagine how much more faith you need to live, if you are not to live in fear and anxiety everyday."

"I can see your point," said the young man.

"And there is one faith which we need most of all," said Miss Henderson. "And that is a faith in God, a Higher Power, Universal Force. It doesn't matter what you call it."

"You're not saying we need faith in God to be happy, are you?" asked the young man.

"I'm not saying you can't be happy without faith in God. What I am saying is that, without it, it is difficult to find lasting happiness. Faith is the foundation for Abundant Happiness. It is like two people who build themselves houses. One builds his house on rock and the other builds his house on sand. Whilst the weather is favorable they'll both be happy, but as soon as a storm comes, the man who built his house on sand will be crushed. Faith is the rock on which lasting happiness is built, it overcomes all adversities, and provides hope and courage to those who have it.

"William James wrote: 'Faith is one of the forces by which men live and the total absence of it means collapse.' And Mahatma Gandhi said, 'Without faith, I should have been a lunatic long ago.' Without faith in a Higher Power, life becomes burdened with doubt, worry, anxiety, and fear. Psychological studies have demonstrated that people with a strong religious faith suffer less depression and stress-related disorders, and cope better with loss. In fact, let me show you this." She reached for a book on the bookcase. It was entitled *Modern Man in Search of a Soul,* by Dr. Carl Jung. "Listen to what Dr. Jung wrote," she said:

Among all my patients in the second half of life—that is to say, over 35—there has not been one whose problem in the last resort was not that of finding a religious outlook on life. It is safe to say that every one of them fell ill because he had lost that which the living religions of every age have given to their followers, and none of them has been really healed who did not regain his religious outlook.

"I understand what you're saying," said the young man. "But, I'm not sure I believe that a God exists."

Miss Henderson thought for a moment. "If I was to tell you that the QE2 ship was formed over millions of years during which time bits of metal and wood and plastic and an assortment of chemicals linked together, you would say I was crazy, wouldn't you?"

"Yes, of course."

"Because you can see that the QE2 has been designed, therefore there must be a designer?"

"Yes," answered the young man.

"When you study the human body, you will see a design far more complex than the QE2," explained Miss Henderson. "For instance, the *Columbia* space shuttle was built with 5.2 million parts, yet the human eye alone has more than one billion parts. Scientists can only marvel at the workings of the human body and despite all our technological advances, we would need a computer the size of the Empire State Building to compare with the human brain.

"Throughout Nature we see incredible design and precision."

"But if there is a God," said the young man, still unconvinced, "Why is there so much misery in the world?"

"You said that a few weeks ago you were unhappy," said Miss Henderson. "Why were you unhappy then, but not now?"

"Because I have learned the secrets of Abundant Happiness," said the young man.

"So if you have the power to create your own happiness, who has the power to create everyone else's?"

"I see what you mean," said the young man. "We are all responsible for our own happiness."

"Of course. So if we are unhappy, it is through our own thoughts and actions. It is not God's doing. To me, this is the most wonderful lesson of the secrets of Abundant Happiness—there is only one person who can make you feel happy or unhappy, and that person is you."

The young man nodded in agreement. "Yes. I suppose it's true."

"In the end," explained Miss Henderson, "faith is something we all need to find for ourselves. But I am a firm believer that if you search for truth, you will find it. And sometimes when we feel most confused and lost, something happens that touches our soul. A little miracle, if you like."

"Such as . . . ?" enquired the young man.

"Such as a chance meeting with an old Chinese man!"

That night, before going to bed, the young man read over the notes he had made that day.

The tenth secret of Abundant Happiness—the power of faith.

Faith is the foundation of Abundant Happiness.
Without faith, there is no lasting happiness.
Faith creates trust, leads to peace of mind, and frees the soul from doubt, worry, anxiety, and fear.

EPILOGUE

He felt the first few drops of rain hit his forehead as he got into his car, and minutes later the storm broke. The thunder and lightning preceded a heavy downpour of rain which beat heavily against the windscreen. His thoughts drifted to the evening, a little over a year ago, when he had met the old Chinese man. He remembered how miserable he had been that evening and smiled as he pictured himself walking back to his car in the wind and rain on that stormy night, unaware that he was about to meet a mysterious man who would change his life forever.

Since that meeting the young man's life had changed immeasurably. He had more energy, more enthusiasm, and was happier than he had ever been. Others noticed it too; there was a sparkle in his eyes, a spring in his step and, more often than not, a smile on his face. Yet he had the same job, he lived in the same apartment, drove the same car, and had the same friends. There was only one thing that had changed in his life . . . and that was himself.

People would often ask him why he always seemed to be so cheerful. On those occasions he would gladly tell the story of his meeting with the old Chinese man and the secrets of Abundant Happiness. It always gave him great pleasure to share what he had learned because he knew it would make a difference in their lives just as it had in his. Many people would phone to thank him and tell him how the secrets had helped them in their lives. And on more than one occasion it had been suggested that he write the story in a book.

Suddenly, there was a loud bang and smoke began rising from under the bonnet of the car. The young man pulled the car over to the side of the road, got out, and walked the two and a half kilometers along the highway to the nearest telephone to call the breakdown service.

As he walked back to his car to wait for a mechanic, he could not help but smile to himself. He became excited, hoping that he might see the old Chinese man leaning against the car, waiting for him as he had done the year before. He wanted to thank the old man and let him know how much the secrets of Abundant Happiness had changed his life. But it was not to be, the old man was not there.

The young man walked round to the driver's door of the car and was about to put the key in the lock when he noticed a bright yellow object lying on the ground. He leaned forward and picked it up.

"Would you believe it?" he whispered to himself. In his hand was a yellow baseball cap!

As he sat in his car waiting for the service mechanic, a thought came to him. He picked up a pen, opened his notebook, and began writing: "It all began one cold and wet October's evening . . . "

Adam J. Jackson is an internationally renowned therapist, author, and motivational speaker. He originally practiced law in England before retraining in natural health sciences. He currently lives in the United Kingdom and heads health clinics both there and in Toronto, Canada.